The View from Here

Craft, Community, and
the Creative Process

Stuart Kestenbaum

Copyright 2012
Brynmorgen Press

For ordering and permissions:
www.brynmorgen.com

Also available for
tablet readers
through iTunes.

ISBN 978-1-929565-45-0

Printed in Hong Kong

This book includes selected poems from the following books:
Pilgrimage from Coyote Love Press,
House of Thanksgiving from Deerbrook Editions,
Prayers and Run-on Sentences from Deerbrook Editions

for Susan, Isaac, and Sam

FOREWORD

Tim McCreight

It was 1988 and I heard that somebody named Stuart Kestenbaum had been hired as the director of the Haystack Mountain School of Crafts. I didn't know him, but the person who told me was a good friend and former neighbor of the guy and he was excited about the decision. I can recall his exact words: "As soon as I heard, I knew it was the right choice. In fact, now that I think about it, the fit is so good there is something inevitable about Stu being the director."

Haystack is a very special place, held in high regard by the thousands of people whose lives have been touched and often altered because of their time there. It was founded in 1951, which coincidentally was the year Stuart Kestenbaum was born. Perched on a rocky ledge on a small island on the Maine coast, Haystack has distinguished itself through its innovative programs, its award-winning architecture, and the consistently high quality of the education that takes place there.

The school owes a great deal to its founding director, a man named Francis Sumner Merritt, who ran the school for 27 years until his retirement in 1978. He created the template for the workshops, helped choose the craft disciplines that would be taught, and oversaw the creation of the current campus. Under his guidance, the cobbled-together dreams of a dozen artists coalesced into a vibrant program. But more than that, Fran Merritt imbued the school with a spirit that runs through every activity, from the breakfast eggs to the late night fireside guitar. People come to Haystack to learn or improve a craft, and often end up learning about things like giving, creativity, and how to draw a clean breath.

Stu Kestenbaum, a potter-turned-poet, had a daunting task ahead when he came to Haystack more than two decades ago. During his tenure as director, he has expanded the school in breadth, depth, and grasp. The school reaches more people in more ways and with greater impact than it ever has before. Under his leadership, it has managed to embrace the concepts and technology of a fast-moving culture while remaining true to its simple roots in ancient craft.

Twice a year, Haystack publishes a newsletter called *Gateway*. In addition to news of the faculty and staff, fundraising announcements, and photos of the rustic campus, each issue of *Gateway* since 1991 has included a feature called "From the Director." These have been gathered into the book you hold in your hands, a chance to reread and perhaps share these gently wise thoughts. Also included here are the texts of speeches Stu Kestenbaum has given at conferences; they are transcribed and available here for the first time.

In these pages readers who have visited Haystack will find sweet reminders of the sun on the deck and the breeze in the towering spruce trees. Those who haven't been on campus will probably get the urge to visit, and yes, it really is that lovely. For all of us, though, these pages provide quiet reminders that for all its complexity, life can be disarmingly simple. A friendly wave to a neighbor, the shared activity of household chores, the haunting lap of waves on a granite shore. In these things we can find wonder and strength.

Each summer Haystack participates in the Fourth of July parade on the Island. The parade and fireworks used to alternate between Deer Isle and Stonington, but now the parade is in Deer Isle and the evening fireworks in Stonington. Stonington is the preferred site for the fireworks, which explode over the water, the sound echoing back from the islands, and Deer Isle is the better side for the parade, with a wider street and better views for spectators.

The parade in Deer Isle makes its way through the town, up to the elementary school and heads back again, so you can enjoy the excitement twice—and it's an exciting event. Walking down the street, with crowds of people—islanders, tourists, summer residents—enthusiastically cheering for floats and walking groups from the community.

For this year's Haystack entry we decided to create the Statue of Liberty. Our work force consisted of some staff, my family, and a handful of students. The Fourth came at the beginning of the third session, so we only had three or four days to get our entry ready for the parade. We made a large papier-mâché head and hands, and created a body out of dyed green sheets. Liberty held aloft a copper torch constructed from sample pieces made by students in Heikki Seppa's metalsmithing workshop who were studying anticlastic raising. We made more torches out of brooms and a sign, reminiscent of a political convention, that said "Haystack: Freedom, Justice, Peace, Equality." We spent two afternoons assembling our Liberty in the sun on the dining hall deck and on the morning of the Fourth loaded it into the school truck and headed to the parade, where we took our place in line with antique cars, a rock band on a flatbed truck, fire engines, the Boy Scouts, and bicyclists who had ridden across the U.S. to raise money for the Island Pantry, which helps provide food for needy families, and others.

Haystack won a trophy—second place in the walking competition, which we added to our growing collection of Fourth of July awards.

The event remains in my mind because of the power of making something and using it right in our community—where people cheered both our message and our efforts—and because of what it says about how we make things. Our parade entry wasn't one person's idea. Someone thought of the big Statue of Liberty, then another person thought of the papier-mâché, and another conceived of how to balance the head on the pole, then the metalsmiths made the torch—each idea led to another and we ended up with something alive—something that grew out of all of our ideas. That this took place with a deadline approaching made it all the more exhilarating.

Robert Frost wrote (in an essay "The Figure a Poem Makes"), "Originality and initiative are all that I ask for my country." I think of that phrase on the Fourth when we use the strengths of craftspeople—imagination and ingenuity—to build something that is more than any one of us.

Spring 1993

Yesterday, following our last substantial snowfall of the winter, a group of families from the Island, probably 25 people in all, went to the Lily Pond in Deer Isle to shovel off some of the ice. Many of you know the Lily Pond as an Island swimming spot, but it's also a serene ice skating location. A three-quarter-mile-long expanse of clear ice rimmed by spruce trees and dotted with skaters and sliders in brightly colored hats and jackets and an occasional careening dog. A scene like this, reminiscent of a Brueghel painting, can make even me feel graceful on skates.

By this point in the snow's life, it had become a compacted six inches. We managed, with one snow blower and 15 shovels, to clear enough ice to skate and play hockey. I'm remembering this today, both through my mind and through the aches in my body. The pond got cleared because of a community effort. It was a bigger job than one person could do, but with a group of people the work went quickly and we all learned from each other, developing a variety of techniques for snow removal.

I'm thinking about this event because it makes me reflect on communities and how they work. A community has a life made up of the lives of its members; it gathers in everything and creates a whole out of it. I've become increasingly aware of this in a community the size of Deer Isle; there is not somebody else, some greater authority that makes things happen—that someone else is you and your neighbors.

Within Deer Isle is the microcosm of Haystack, an even smaller community, and a temporary one at that; one that comes together and quickly gains a sense of itself and its members. Each community that is formed during our workshops is unique, but they all share in common the sense of momentum in investigating ideas and taking chances with those ideas. We all learn from each other in a context like this. And when you look back at the end of a session and see what the community has accomplished, it always seems much greater than what you thought was possible. Just like when we looked back at the cleared ice yesterday; there we were, a group of people with shovels and an idea, and in time, after a community effort and a sore back or two, we were gliding along in another world.

This February, architect Edward Larrabee Barnes and Haystack were recognized by the American Institute of Architects with its Twenty-Five Year Award. This award, which is given annually, "celebrates the enduring nature of design excellence." Other buildings that have received the honor include Rockefeller Center, Dulles International Airport, Gateway Arch in St. Louis, and the Guggenheim Museum. I traveled down to Washington, D.C. to attend the gala event, which included not only the announcement of the Twenty-Five Year Award, but also honored awards in architecture and urban design to newer buildings, and a gold medal award to British architect Sir Norman Foster.

A journey that begins in Deer Isle is always a reminder that we're not centrally located. There's the early morning 60-mile ride in the dark on an icy road to Bangor, the windy take-off in a tiny plane, a change of planes in Boston, the wait, and the connection to Washington. You can begin your morning at 5:30 in Deer Isle and arrive in Washington by 2:30. The flight gives me a tremendous view of the Maine coast, the awesome expanse of ocean, and then the sprawl of human activity from Boston through Philadelphia, Baltimore, and Washington. From the air I can spot Camden Yards, the Baltimore Orioles' new ballpark (and one of the winners of this year's

honor awards). Arriving in Washington, waiting for the Metro to bring me into the city, I look like any other traveler, but in my mind I am carrying the places I've come from and the landscapes I've seen.

The evening is black tie, definitely not the standard Haystack outfit. The only other time I wore a tuxedo I was a senior in high school, so I feel more like I'm in a costume than in my clothes, but in the evening I'm standing in the National Building Museum with about 700 other people, looking remarkably like everyone else. Following a dinner, the awards presentations begin. And there, on a large screen is a Haystack video, which the AIA had produced for the event. The tape, which runs 6 minutes, gives a clear sense of the site and architecture and the impact the school has on people.

It's a thrilling moment in the urban night, to see our modest wooden buildings recognized with this award, to see our shingles and decks, spruce and lichen, and to hear Ed Barnes talk (in the video) of his response to the site and hear students talk about the impact the architecture has on their work. The buildings work doubly well because, in addition to being integrated into the site, they convey what the best of the crafts can impart. There is the human scale, the sense of a seemingly intuitive grace, and a thoughtful relationship to the earth. It's a small victory for humility.

Fall 1994

A year and a half ago I asked Wayne Higby to teach a workshop in ceramics. Wayne, a loyal supporter and friend of Haystack, is always eager to be involved with the school. He also likes to push limits. He wanted to teach, but wanted to try something new. He thought it over for a few days and said he would teach if I would teach with him; we would design a workshop that would address ceramics and writing. Wanting to have Wayne teach again, and thinking it could be exciting to take a risk with this, I agreed.

I then placed my upcoming role of teacher in the appropriate file folder in my mind and went on with my directorial responsibilities. But from time to time, with some nervousness and anticipation, I would remember my commitment. In December as we were preparing the catalog, in March when we reviewed applications, and in April when we began to re-open the school, I wondered how I would juggle the roles of director and teacher, and what it would be like to participate fully in a single workshop, to see Haystack from the perspective of a teacher.

For me it turned out to be a wonderful experience, improvising with Wayne and teaching supportive students who were willing to take risks. We wrote and made things, using language as a way to inform our work in clay. In preparation for the season, I developed some exercises to use with the class. One of these was to write about a work of art—your own or somebody else's—to go inside it and make discoveries through writing. I wrote about a piece of Wayne's that I had long admired—a large raku-fired landscape bowl. Writing this was a thrilling journey that allowed me to see the work in a new way. Sometimes re-examining those things and ideas that you're familiar with allows you to know them again. Teaching here was like that; it gave me a renewed sense of Haystack and its mission.

After Floating Rocks Beach
a large landscape bowl by Wayne Higby

The sky is round, curving
into the rim of the world,
the edge of things. It is
the gentle curve of your arm
holding up the edge
of this planet, wrapped
in a circle like a dancer,
or the way a mother loves a child
with her forearm and elbow,
the crook to nestle in.
This landscape comes
from another time, the rocks
were towed by
boats in the foggy night.
They float in front of us.
At first you think these stones
are from a Renaissance painting,
that they were behind the annunciation
of the miraculous birth
and have floated here before your eyes.
Then you hear the wind,
a steady wind that catches
in the crevice of your ears
the perpetual sound we are adrift in
the sound before sound had a name.

This fall and winter newspapers and national magazines were filled with information on computers—multi-media CD-ROM, the internet, laptop-docking stations—the high-tech future had arrived for consumers. At Haystack we've been computerized since the early 1980s. All of our donor and attendance records are on computers as is our mailing list. Our back-up system, though, is decidedly handmade.

We keep separate 3 x 5 index card files with the addresses, attendance and donor information, on all students and contributors. Whenever someone makes a donation to the school, that's the card we look at when we send our letters of thanks. Each card tells a story. With some I can recognize Fran Merritt's handwriting in the address, and the address corrections and notes by Ethel Clifford, Howard Evans, and Candy Haskell. I pass through generations of technology—from the handwritten card to a typed gum label to the electric typewriter. I can see students who later became teachers, and people who first came to Haystack as college students; I follow the crossed-out addresses on the cards as they move three or four times to their current residences. The cards also tell a story of the financial support people have given. Some begin in the top right hand corner with a gift in the 1970s and continue through 1995, running down the side of the card over to the back. One of our donors had been here as a student in 1957, and made his first contribution this year.

When I look at these cards, it's as if I'm having a conversation with these friends and supporters. Some people I know very well and seeing the cards brings back memories of past workshops; others I know only through their donations. Either way, though, when I'm holding the cards in my hands, it's an immediate connection.

I know that all this information is stored on our computers, but there is something tangible in the dog-eared index cards of old friends, filed alongside the crisp new cards of last summer's first time students. It struck me when we were inundated with the news of the computerized future that these cards were another manifestation of a Haystack spirit and what makes craft compelling to us. They tell a human story that you can touch, that you can hold in your hands.

Fall 1995

When we end our programming year in October, it's a time when I can look back on an entire six-month season filled with the remarkable creative energy of the Haystack community. And it's a season where the facility is in use nearly every day—from conferences and short workshops in the spring and fall to our two- and three-week sessions of summer. Each day has moments that stand out as exemplars of what it is that Haystack does best as an educational institution.

During our first session in June, Mary Law was teaching a pottery workshop. Mary Law, a Chattanooga, Tennessee native who still retains her southern lilt after many years in Northern California, is called by both her first and last names as if they were one. She's a gracious and skilled potter and teacher. During the same session, potter Karen Karnes came by for a visit and spoke with Mary Law's class. Mary Law told me she was thrilled, because many years before when she was a beginning student in a workshop at Penland, Karen had been her teacher. She recalled that Karen had taken her aside near the end of the workshop and told her she "had what it took" to become a potter and that she should devote herself to that life. In the midst of an intensive workshop, it was a pivotal moment, one that gave Mary Law the courage to pursue a life as a maker. What Karen had given was encouragement, and what an impact a little encouragement can have.

That's what happens in every workshop at Haystack in some form or another—the encouragement to try something new, to develop a new idea, to think in a way you hadn't thought before. This encouragement may come from a teacher, fellow student, or within yourself. It may happen in a workshop, in a conversation over dinner, seeing slides of someone's work, in a walk on the shore. It may happen to a beginning artist, an advanced professional, an 18- or 85-year old.

There was a wonderful sense of continuity in hearing Karen speak with Mary Law's students. I realized in Mary Law's own workshop there would be similar moments of encouragement that would, in turn, engender future moments of encouragement. It's these moments that lead us forward into our lives.

There is an old saying that there are only two seasons in Maine—winter and the Fourth of July. Those of us who have spent remarkably clear days on the Haystack decks know that this isn't completely true, but there are definitely two Haystack seasons—when you're here and when you're not. During the spring, summer, and fall when the studios are active and the dining room is full of people engaged in conversations, there doesn't seem to ever have been a time when we weren't alive in a session. When we close down for the season, though, and move back to our winter quarters in Deer Isle village, it's a decidedly quieter world, warmer in winter but without the view, and also without the immediate sense of community that Haystack holds when it is open.

But the community that Haystack has engendered has not gone away, it's just far-flung, and we reconvene in smaller ways, by postcard and letter, fax and phone. No e-mail yet, but soon. Whatever the form, these connections are what remind us of what happens at Haystack and why it's important. Nearly every week we'll receive show announcements from workshop leaders and students, work that may have begun as an experiment at Haystack. One show announcement in November came with a note "you know Haystack makes it all worth it, things just seem to make sense." Other times we'll receive snapshots taken during a session and are transported back to one of those ice-less days. And then there are the flash photos where our red eyes glow and we look as if were all possessed by some sort of spirit, which I suppose we were.

Winter is also when we receive requests for information about Haystack, the way that people order seed catalogs, with hope for a time of planting and growth. Earlier this month a woman called who told me she had graduated from the School for American Craftsmen majoring in textiles. She had become a textile designer and had always told herself that by the time she was 60 she would come to Haystack. She had recently celebrated her 60th birthday and was ready to take a weaving workshop. I felt an immediate connection, as if she had carried a potential Haystack with her for nearly 40 years.

And I suppose in the winter, in a way, we're all carrying that potential community within us, the one from the past that can carry us forward in our work and the one that may come this year, opening up a world we can't yet imagine.

Most of you probably know Haystack through our programs in June, July, and August. Our entire season, though, runs from mid-May through mid-October. We move out to the campus when there are only buds on the trees, and move back to our winter office when autumn is at peak color, the yellow maples' leaves brilliant against the dark green spruce. We stretch our season in the unheated studios just about as far as we can.

Spring and fall are busy times for us. We have shorter workshops for high school students and New England and Maine residents. This year we added an additional program—New Works—a retreat session for former Haystack faculty to pursue ideas for new projects. We also host college and other professional groups. Our short sessions possess a great intensity. They are all five days or less in length and the activity is more of a sprint than a long distance run. The character of discovery, though, does not differ from our longer workshops.

One of the more recent programs, Studio Based Learning, begun in 1992, brings together high school students from Deer Isle-Stonington High School and George Stevens Academy (the Blue Hill high school) for a four-day workshop. The rhythm of the studios is similar to our summer programs, with the exception that we make sure everyone is in bed by 11:30. And 70 high school students consume an unbelievable amount of hot chocolate.

One comment from this year's Studio Based Learning session stands out in my mind. When we asked students, as part of our evaluation, what was most difficult for them about their studio work, one young woman in printmaking wrote "getting ideas [when] I ran out [of them], but once I did [get ideas] they were back for good."

For high school students who are used to 45- or 80-minute classes, a full Haystack day devoted to art opens up a whole other way of looking at work. They have the time for all the experiments and failures that are critical to learning. It's the kind of time that exists for all of us who have taken workshops at Haystack. I think of it as a different time zone, one where you can try out new ideas, give up on them, come back to them renewed, or discover that you have changed the way that you are looking at your work.

Those moments may be small in terms of all the waking hours that we have in our lives, but to know that they are there can give us a kind of faith in our ability to explore our art. When we fear there is nothing left, we can dig deeper and discover there is more to perplex and enlighten us.

Last fall we began work on the expansion of our library and store, which will now be a new wing of the Gateway Building. We've undertaken the construction of this with our own staff, and because the winter has been virtually snowless, building continued through January. Haystack has a tremendously talented and resourceful maintenance crew. This project has been headed up by our studio technician, Jonathan Doolan, assisted by Gene Koch (from our maintenance staff), and Frank Pitcher (our studio coordinator). Tom Smith (our cook), Al Chapman (Haystack student and Island carpenter), and J. Fred Woell (head of maintenance) also helped in October and November.

Haystack's creativity goes beyond its studios, and making a building is certainly a creative act. Everyday this crew made aesthetic and technical decisions and found innovative solutions to the challenges of working on the coast of Maine in the winter. Their creative spirit went beyond their work, too.

Both Jonathan and Gene are avid skaters. When the weather turned cold enough to make ice, they decided, along with Frank, to build a rink on the main deck. They recycled some 2 x 4s and took a large blue tarp that had been used to cover the library roof, creating a 1,250 square foot rink, nearly covering the entire deck. We had the same astounding view of Jericho Bay, a view elevated by the extra inches that ice and skates provide. With the blue tarp underneath the ice, the whole rink had the look of an enormous synthetic ice pack. Right where we eat our lunches in the summer, we could glide and practice turns, kind of a Rockefeller Center Downeast, with spruce trees moving in the steady wind.

A few years back one of our instructors, commenting on a new program, wrote to me that she was glad to see that Haystack was "still a work in progress," and between the construction and the impromptu rink, we certainly were one this winter. I was heartened when she wrote that, because what higher praise can there be than to be a work in progress? Whether it's renovating a building or developing a new program, being a work in progress means that you are alive as an institution. Haystack is now in its fifth decade, mature enough to have developed systems and traditions that carry it forward. And certainly systems are imperative for a non-profit organization to survive and remain strong; so we budget, we plan, we raise funds, we run our programs, we keep shingling and repairing.

In a sense, though, Haystack's greatest strength is that it reinvents itself every time a workshop begins, every time someone tries out a new idea in a studio, every time someone wants to skate in the middle of the winter. We begin with the empty space and ask you to come and transform it with your ideas, with what moves you to create.

Fall 1997

I'm writing this in mid-October, during our Open Door workshop, our final event of the season. Sometimes we call Haystack a summer program, but our "summer" is really half a year long. It begins with weekend workshops in mid-May, followed by our two- and three-week long summer sessions and on to a fall that is full of shorter workshops. Open Door is specifically for Maine craftspeople; a workshop this time of year is perhaps most appropriate for year-round residents of northern New England. While the daytime temperatures can be in the sixties, it can get quite a bit chillier at night. Nine years ago it snowed and the power to the island was knocked out. I remember looking around the dining hall then and everyone was bulked up with many layers of clothing—like an instant weight gain. But usually it's just brisk autumnal weather, with a markedly shorter day than in the summer. When we gather for dinner, the sun is already setting—quite a difference from June when there is still light in the sky at 9 pm.

There is a beautifully austere quality to the light here as we move toward the later fall and winter. The days take on a more introspective and reflective feel for me. When the dining hall is full for dinner on these final nights of our year, I can look back and see not just the faces from this session, but the many sessions since we began in May. While a big part of the world of

Haystack takes place in the studios, there is an equal part that takes place at meal times.

It's not just that we are nourished or that we don't have to cook and can give ourselves over to thinking about our artwork. It's the way that gathering around the tables, and sharing our food in common makes a community out of the different studios, different ages, different countries, and different interests. Sometimes looking around the room at the animated conversations taking place around the pine tables, I feel that I can look back beyond this season or the past few years, right back to the first gatherings of the school when it moved to this site in 1961. The hair and clothing styles have changed, tofu was not on the menu, but in many ways we remain the same. There is the dining room with the stunning horizon spreading about before us, and we are nourished by what we are imagining together.

Spring 1998 _____

I am sure that many of you followed the news this January of the severe ice storms in Maine—some of you by living through it. On Deer Isle we didn't suffer as much as other parts of the state; being closer to the ocean kept us warmer, making for less freezing rain. Our grass was matted with ice, though, built up over three days of precipitation, and the birches were leaning with the growing, heavy weight. Off island many hardwoods snapped off at the tops, limbs were everywhere; power lines lay across the roads and the birch saplings bent over all the way to the ground.

Some towns and cities in Maine lost power for more than a week. On Deer Isle we were fortunate to be without power for only 2½ days. What's most remarkable about the experience to me was the silence of it. A home without power is a quieter place—no hum of the refrigerator's compressor, no cycling on and off of the oil furnace or the sound of baseboard heat moving through a room, no news on the radio and TV, no fan running in the computer. After two flushes of the toilets, no more sound of water in the house either. It's similar to camping out, except that in your home you're keenly aware of the contrast with what you normally have a your disposal.

As the evening fell the first night, and we lit candles and kerosene lamps, I felt a kinship with those who spent winters here without electricity; my own home, built around 1840, has existed longer without power than with it. The sense of the early winter darkness is more profound, and I grew much more aware of my use of resources—light, heat, and water. It's not exactly suffering—we ate all the quickly softening ice cream from the freezer while playing "Clue" by candlelight—but it's a heightened awareness of what we have and what we have lost.

The silence reminded me, too, of the silence of making a pot. The quiet air inside the vessel, the hushed moment of relationship between the clay and me, the form that evolves, the connection between my body and something that carries an ancient history within itself.

— *Fall 1998* ——————————————

This year marks the end of my tenth year at Haystack. Some mornings when I stand on the main deck and look out to the islands it feels like it's my first day here, but there are many signs that time has passed. When I began I could easily carry either one of my sons on my shoulders. Now the older one stands at eye level with me. I've followed the careers of people who came here first as students and who now are teaching workshops for us. Shingles that were new are now weathering to gray; others have been replaced and have the brightness that the entire campus must have had when it opened in 1961.

Large spruce trees have blown down in winter winds, and thousands of seedlings have taken root in the thin soil. We've replaced kilns and glass furnaces, in some cases more than once. We've added onto the buildings and built some new ones as well. Deck boards have come and gone, cut up and warming us in the dining hall fireplace.

Sometimes in the spring when we rip out the old boards, replace a roof or re-shingle, I think that in 100 years we will have replaced all the wood on campus; no part of it would be original then, but it would still, I am sure, retain the original spirit. It's the same way that, even though every workshop begins anew, each also has a remarkable similarity.

For me it's a spirit of discovery. That discovery includes the adventure of finding the place for the first time and learning new techniques. Then come the more subtle discoveries made by venturing into the unknown place of creation and coming back with something we didn't know existed—a voice, an idea, a way of seeing. Watching so many of you set forth on those journeys of discovery makes time—even ten years—pass in a way that's both slow and fast, that's renewed and alive.

Spring 1999

Last week I traveled to New York—the perfect time of year for me to see museums, galleries, movies, and visit with friends. Once our programs start in May, I rarely make it over the bridge. I love the way the urban world of Manhattan makes a nature of its own. The yellow cabs on a gray day on Lexington Avenue are like flowing water; the brick, stone, and glass of the built environment make their own nearly organic rhythm with one another. And to visit museums that hold so much knowledge. On one side of Central Park, the Metropolitan Museum of Art with its incredible abundance of our cultural heritage. On the other side of the park, the Museum of Natural History with its 100 million year old dinosaur bones. Outside, pigeons and sparrows—the descendants of those dinosaurs—roost in the trees.

On the way back from New York we visited some friends in Boston and went to Walden Pond. I had never been to Walden before, and my friends warned me not to expect Henry David Thoreau's pristine Walden, but a well-used swimming spot with a large parking lot close by. Perhaps because I grew up in New Jersey, the parking lot didn't seem that large, and, with the exception of a park building, the pond is undeveloped. I can't imagine, though, that Thoreau could have ever envisioned that Boston would sprawl toward Concord the way that it does, or that so many people would visit Walden Pond—tens of thousands a year—that the trails would begin to erode because of our footsteps trying to follow his footsteps.

At the edge of the parking lot stood a replica of the cabin that Thoreau built, where he had gone to "live deliberately." Even though the cabin was removed from the site of the original one that was closer to the pond, it was thrilling to see it. What is most striking is the scale of it—10' x 15'—large enough to hold a bed, a stove, and a table. Think of the ideas that were born in that one simple place.

It also made me reflect on another modest structure—our Haystack cabins. When the school's architect Edward Larrabee Barnes visited us last year, he told me when we were touring the cabins that his goal had been simplicity: "basic living and high thinking" was how Ed described it to the school's trustees back in 1960. I'd say that Ed's description back then was pretty apt. Perhaps while I was visiting Walden someone walked up the icy Haystack road and looked at our studios and cabins, the lichen growing on cedar shingles, the February wind rattling the gray doors.

—— *Fall 1999* ————————————————————

During the Haystack season I don't stray too far from Deer Isle. This August, though, at the beginning of our sixth session, I took a short but extraordinary journey to North Haven Island. Although I've lived in Maine for 25 years, I had never traveled to North Haven, 12 miles offshore, east of Deer Isle, with a year-round population of 350. Eric Hopkins, North Haven native, who was teaching a drawing and painting workshop that session, invited me along with Jonathan Doolan, our studio technician, to fly to North Haven from Stonington, so that Eric could pick up his 19 foot boat and motor back to Haystack.

We were driven in the Haystack truck to the Stonington airport, where we met our charter plane—a single-engine Cessna that holds 4. Our young pilot told us, as we sat in a space that's smaller than a big closet, that the plane had two emergency exits and that we would find a diagram of this in the seat pouch. I thought of the Big Bopper, Bully Holley and Richie Valens.

But we took off gracefully and flying over Deer Isle at an altitude of 1000 feet, elevated above the roads and landmarks that I know so well, it was a map come to life. It's as if map had been a foreign language I studied and now I was in a country where it was spoken and lived. North Haven, via car and ferry, is a journey of 3 hours; by plane, it's 10 minutes. We landed on a grass runway, tall spruce trees on either side, and walked to Eric's home. From there we rode with his family to the harbor and boarded the boat.

Threading his way around the abundant lobster buoys of the Fox Island Thorofare and then into a breezy Penobscot Bay, Eric brought us back to Haystack, the chop of the waves slapping against the hull of the boat. The lobstermen who fish these waters can see the unity of the islands, a world read by ledges, currents, and tides. By water, our islands are neighbors; the trip back took a little more than 30 minutes. We headed for Mark Island Light, a location that inspired painter John Marin, and then through the Deer Isle Thorofare, past the mostly un-inhabited islands that a century ago were farmed or quarried, to Sheep Island, and into Western Cove, where Haystack is located. All in all, between the flight, a brief visit on North Haven, and a boat ride, we departed in the late afternoon and arrived back at school in time for dinner.

Eric wanted to have the boat here so he could take his students out on the water and they could see the landscape in a new way. The journey had done the same for me. What a world I had seen in those few hours. First the aerial view, looking at the land without signs, without borders and the endless spread of the ocean on the horizon, and then back by water, a

reminder of the common heritage that all the islands in this part of the world share, how we are united by history and geology. For a brief moment, Deer Isle was cut loose from the bridge as well.

It was a world where we made our way without roads. The roads around here I've memorized. I know where the surface heaves with frost in the winter, where the deer are likely to run out from the shoulders, and where the sharp curves come up suddenly. But in that roadless journey I could see our world tied together in a new way. It's similar, I think, to how we are seeing when we create; it's not the world we thought we were going to see, it's the world that's waiting to be seen, that's being discovered in every moment.

In the middle of the summer I'm sometimes asked, "what do you do in the winter?" I usually just answer "get ready for the summer," which has for me a nice symmetry about it and a kind of Maine brevity as well. What we actually do in the winter, in addition to watching it get dark early, is plan for our future. A part of this is making presentations about Haystack to prospective students in different parts of the country.

This winter I traveled to California, where I spoke at four university programs. I'm not a frequent visitor to the other coast; and the only other time I was in California was when I was in college and one summer a friend and I drove someone's three-speed Toyota Corolla from New Jersey to San Francisco, and hitch-hiked back. I can still remember every ride we got, particularly the sputtering Volkswagen bus that took us all the way through Nevada and Wyoming.

William Carlos Williams in his poem "January Morning," says that "the beauties of travel are due to/ the strange hours we keep to see them," and at 7:00 in the morning, when it's barely light out, I'm walking across the tarmac to the small plane at the Bangor airport carrying my luggage, including the slides that I'll be showing later that day all the way across the country. It's a luminescent world, the gray day growing lighter and the runway surrounded by huge mounds of snow, plowed up the night before.

When I know I'm going to be talking about Haystack, I feel in some way as if I'm carrying the school with me—I think about the kind of community it is and can't help contrasting it with the world of airports and planes, where I overhear cell phone conversations I wish I hadn't and am served peanuts and more peanuts and snacks in boxes. It's a relief when I reach California and visit the different schools, and see how they are anchored in their communities. I meet people who've been students and teachers here, and after a few moments the memories of those sessions are with me. I meet people who I can envision as participants in next year's workshops and think of them making the trek I've just made in the opposite direction.

And then I show the slides, images of islands and water, granite and spruce, the campus, the studios, and the faculty who will be teaching in the coming summer. I project an image of the desserts disappearing, and one of the full dining hall at dinner time. When that slide appears I talk about students last year ranging in age from 18 to 91, how people came from 38 states and 14 countries. And I talk about the scale—only 85-90 people at any one time—and how quickly people get to know one another.

After traveling 3,000 miles, after the car rental agent trying to sell me more insurance than I need, after the steady whoosh and hum of the freeway, looking at this image on the screen I am struck by the smallness and the bigness of it all at once. It's a small scale but a big idea. That people come together to form a community of artists where risk and invention are central. That people share food and ideas and your studio is always open and only a short walk away.

Fall 2000

I am writing this during the next to last day of our programming season—our Open Door workshop for Maine residents held over the Columbus Day weekend. As I'm working at the computer in my cabin, small heater at my feet and hands nearly numb at the keyboard, it seems an appropriate, if slightly cold time, to reflect on our season, which stretches from early May to the middle of October.

One of the first programs of the Haystack season is the Student Craft Institute, a three-day workshop for Maine high school juniors, selected by their art teachers. We have 72 students from as many different high schools from throughout the state. For many, their experience at Haystack is their first opportunity to work among peers in an intensive workshop format in a place dedicated to making art.

As part of our evaluation we ask participants to describe Haystack to someone who has never been here before. This spring one student wrote that Haystack was "an artistic oxygen tank" and "some wacky art community school thing," descriptions that were both vivid and appropriate.

I'm sure that we must be providing artistic oxygen here. How else to explain those days that stretch from early morning to late evening and beyond, when the world is full of possibility? How else to explain the intense focus that people bring to their work, and the amount of work that they can accomplish in two or three weeks?

Those days and weeks can seem endless, not in the way a few hours wait at an airport can seem endless, but in the way that time can be without time when we slow down and examine who we are and what we are making. And in that slow time something happens: we might try something new and have multiple failures leading to one sweet success. We might come to look at our work in a way that will take us beyond what we had imagined before.

Next year this "wacky art community school thing" will celebrate its 50th year. For 40 years now students and teachers have come from all over the U.S. and abroad to work in our studios, to share ideas, to improvise, to have conversations. Whether it's an intensive workshop in May that may mark the beginning of a budding art career for a high school student, or a two-week session with students from Europe, Asia, and the U.S. in the clear blue light of August, I am always amazed at the kind of learning that takes place. It's a stunningly simple idea—bring people together from varied backgrounds, give them time, space, and food and foster a community. This concept has produced some remarkable results both for individual makers and for the entire craft field.

As an institution that is nearing 50, it seems to me a wonderful compliment that we can be defined as wacky. I'm not exactly sure what a teen definition of wacky is, but in this context I infer it to mean that we are not doctrinaire, that we can take chances, try new things, and be always alive in a world that combines materials and ideas in surprising ways.

Just after Christmas we received the sad news that Fran Merritt had passed away. Fran was the guiding spirit behind Haystack from its first session in 1951 until he retired in 1977. It's hard to conceive of Haystack as we know it without seeing the impact of his vision. The sense of community that he created and the innovative programming he pioneered, shaped the school. Fran's vision was accompanied by a gracious touch. His ability to encourage people at all levels to pursue those things that inspired them is legendary.

Fran's sense of experimentation included both the programs that he developed at the school—European and African sessions, collaborations with architects and writers, programs for high school students—and his own artwork as well. As a printmaker he used anything he could get his hands on—thermo fax paper, incised plaster, and gelatin plates to create work that is both evocative and lyrical.

After his retirement, Fran devoted his time to working in his studio and also taught at Haystack and in other programs. I first came to know him as a teacher in 1984, when I worked for the Maine Arts Commission. He was a visiting artist at the Maine Correctional Center where my wife, Susan Webster, was an artist in residence and directed the art program, which was housed in a converted cellblock. Fran and ten inmates had created a 3' x 6' gelatin plate on a worktable. They were trying to make "the world's largest gelatin print." Climbing on the table as people placed sheets of paper down on the surface, Fran engaged everyone in the planning and execution of the piece. He had the ability to create this kind of controlled and magical chaos in his teaching, where he and his students could become lost in their investigations and end up in a different place from where they had started.

Until they moved to Belfast, Maine four years ago, Fran and his wife Priscilla were our neighbors, too. We shared the kinds of small experiences that neighbors do. He would look after our cats when we were away, and we kept track of one another's comings and goings and shared an occasional meal. Fran came over for our son Isaac's 11th birthday wearing a new top hat, old canvas tennis sneakers, and the tails that he wore at his wedding 55 years earlier. I keep that image in my mind as a manifestation of his playful elegance.

When I first became director, Fran told me a story of a Maine school superintendent who visited the Deer Isle campus and looked at the wooden buildings descending the rocky slope. "What's all this temporary construction?" he asked, to which Fran quickly replied, "well the buildings are temporary but the concept is permanent."

And what a legacy that concept is! That we can become a part of a community where creativity and experimentation are honored, where we can ask questions about ourselves and our work not knowing where it will lead, where the work of the hand and the rhythm of the tides live side by side.

By the time that you read this perhaps the heart of the world will be beating differently, but I am writing this a few weeks after the attacks on the World Trade Center and the Pentagon, and the memories of September 11 are still raw and unreal.

That day on Deer Isle was one of those clear autumnal days with an impossibly blue sky and clear refined light. We were in the middle of a program for high school students from Deer Isle and the Blue Hill Peninsula. This program, Studio Based Learning, is an intensive residential program similar to other Haystack programs; kids who normally have 50 minutes to work on an idea are given the opportunity to work all day and all night.

We had completed one day of our three-day session when we received word of the attack. The news came in over the radio in the kitchen shortly after breakfast and our horror grew as we received more information. We decided to let all the students in the studios know, and gathered everyone on the deck just before lunch. It seemed important for us to go on with our program. I spoke with the students briefly about the events and urged them, as our way of responding at that moment, that they be peaceful people and make beautiful things. How small all our efforts can seem at a moment like that. We stood in a circle and then Gerry Williams, who was teaching a clay workshop, spoke eloquently about rooting out the seeds of hatred where they have been sown.

My own anguish was more personal. I had not heard any word concerning my brother, Howard, who worked at the World Trade Center. My brilliant older brother, the idol of my elementary school years, the loving father and husband, a kind, generous, and gentle spirit.

We continued through that day and into the next. We were far away from the world and connected to it at the same time. How poignant the act of making is amidst the destruction and atrocity we had witnessed. And all the more moving that our students were boys and girls, just beginning to make their way in the world, working at the loom, the potter's wheel, the forge, those ancient tools of creation.

Just before the end of the workshop I received the devastating news that my brother was among those who perished. Where to go with such loss and grief? It happened that my wife, Susan Webster, and our younger son, Sam, were both at the school. Susan was teaching printmaking and Sam was taking the clay workshop. As we removed ourselves from the group to begin our mourning as a family, we decided to go for a walk to the ocean. Sam, intuitive and compassionate beyond his 16 years, grabbed a handful of clay.

When we reached the shore, Sam gave us each some clay and we began to make cups. As we formed the clay, the surface quickly dried and cracked. A vessel for grief, I thought. We worked in silence and made one hole in each pot so that grief

could drain out. We placed these pieces on the barnacles at the edge of the granite ledge, just out of reach of the incoming tide. We watched together as the water—a whole ocean of tears and life—lapped up and took into itself what we had made.

Spring 2002

We all know we can't have too many expectations of the weather, particularly in New England, where weather can change its mind at least a few times a day. This winter has been particularly confusing. Some days have brought a welcome, blustery cold, while other days have been like the spring thaw or late November, a landscape of small piles of snow mixed with gravel and fallen leaves. It has made for a season where I can't tell if it's just beginning or just ending.

We rely on seasons to anchor us. We can recognize in our bodies that the light of June is different from the light in December. It's how we stay in tune with our planet spinning in the cosmos. On Deer Isle we also stay in tune with a Haystack year, which has its own seasons. When our programming year is ending in October, we've already planned the next year's sessions and are editing the workshop descriptions. In January, we're mailing thousands of course brochures all across the country like so many seed catalogs, and you get to look over the summer offerings, just the way you might plan a garden, dreaming of what might take root and blossom inside you and your work.

Then your applications begin to arrive, some from exotic locations, some from just around the corner, and something in us begins to awaken. Still, it's hard to believe that these pieces of paper will actually mean that in four or five months the studios will be full of familiar and unfamiliar faces, animated conversations, and new ideas. Next we're coaxing the buildings back to life, turning on the water, making repairs, and adding new equipment. Then, as if it has never happened before, our students and faculty begin to arrive and we're alive again, breathing the air of art and community. You have been approaching your arrival in the same way, first as a thought, then as a plan, and finally as a luggage-and-supply-hauling reality.

In this way the season and our own intentions have come together, and it is always a wonderful, surprising and nearly miraculous moment to behold. Each phase of this process has its time and its place. Here and elsewhere this year, I think it's not only winter that has been unsettled, but our own creative lives as well. Do we turn to art to heal ourselves and others? Can we make something that will make sense of events that don't make sense? We know that the life of each emotion, each idea, each yearning, has its own rhythm, as does the natural world that has formed and shaped us. We have times of excitement, clarity, confusion, silence, and making, sometimes weeks and months apart, sometimes a split second apart. When the time is right, we slide open the gray doors to the studio, roll up our sleeves and get to work.

Fall 2002

How lucky I am for six months of the year to work in an office with such a spectacular view—Jericho Bay and the spruce covered islands, the perfect curve of the horizon where the Atlantic meets the sky. Sometimes from our office window I feel as if I'm at the helm on the bridge of a ship and we're sailing off into those waters, joining the lobster boats and schooners that pass by us everyday. It seems the appropriate metaphor for Haystack too, since the time in the studio has the intensity of a voyage, how we're all joined together heading for some unknown land. Whether we're here for three days or three weeks, the sense of exploration and discovery permeates everything that happens.

Each studio can be its own vessel too, heading into the wind, with the bright sun reflecting off the water, or at night with its light spreading into the darkness. One session this summer the glass class led by Josiah McElheny and Jan Erik Ritzman headed off on a real boat—the theme of the workshop was to make vessels for a voyage. So the entire group made items to take with them—bottles to hold liquid, glass horns to play, cups and goblets to drink from—and packed up provisions in wooden crates they built themselves. The destination was an uninhabited island farther south, where they would spend the day using what they had made. A practical and metaphorical journey all at once.

We drove in the school truck to the dock in Oceanville and carried the supplies in the fully loaded crates down the ramp, made steep by the low tide. This was an international crew—students and teachers from Sweden, Japan, Denmark, Norway, and the U.S. The crates reminded me of ancient cargoes, amphorae for wine and oil, as if our sailors would be setting off across the Mediterranean a few thousand years ago. I took photos of everyone in the lobster boat, undid the lines, and waved good-bye.

I returned to the campus, thinking about all the stages of our journeys of discovery that take place in the workshops—excitement, confusion, elation, knowledge—and how they all mix together and we find ourselves in a different place from where we started. Then I walked past the kiln deck, the two gas kilns cooling with the doors part-way open—still 250 degrees or more inside—and the pots pinging as they cooled, like something returned from outer space. I remembered when I was a potter, how fire changed things, how I stood near kilns in that same spot over twenty-five years ago, laughing, exhilarated, dirty with clay, my hands learning a new language, unloading the still warm pots, each small vessel a discovery and a beginning.

Every winter we send the Haystack catalog to students, faculty, friends, and prospective students. For me this mailing is the official beginning of the Haystack year. We gather a crew at the winter office—where everyone can catch up on the latest Island news—stick mailing labels with your name and thousands of other names on the fresh-from-the printer catalogs, load up the large, heavy bags, and drive down to the Deer Isle post office. There we are at the end of January, an icy wind blowing off the water, a group of us unloading the bags into bins, which get trucked to Bangor and then sent out into the world. The catalog makes its way to every state in the U.S. and Asia, Africa, the Americas, and Europe.

Thinking of our modest publication in the mail stream is a humbling kind of experience; to us it's a vital piece of information about the future of crafts, while to the letter carriers it's just another two ounces that's sandwiched between sales flyers, magazines, and bills. I like the plain white outside of the catalog and the inside view of the Haystack campus, that view that always astounds us whether it's our first time taking a workshop or we work here everyday. Inside are the descriptions of the summer's workshops. It's a world of potential that won't come to life until each session begins.

Our mailing arrives just about the same time that the seed catalogs arrive, and perhaps there's a similar function. In the deep freeze of winter you can dream of something flowering, dream of all that your garden can be this year. And, like a packet of seeds, each of our workshops is a kind of artistic agriculture—we're planting ideas. Who knows what will germinate and break through the soil and what will take root and thrive. Perhaps you'll decide to enroll for a workshop this year, or you may tell a friend or student, or you may just remember one that you took here and the impact that it had on you and your work.

When the school is open and the workshops are alive with conversations and laughter, the connection between Haystack and you is obvious. And, while we appreciate the quiet of our winter, it's the time when our connection to you is less tangible. Sending the catalog reconnects us. Our humble catalog makes its remarkable journey, finding its way from Deer Isle to your home, probably with fewer wrong turns and flights delays than what you experience on your way here. You come home from work or from your studio, you sort through the day's mail and there we are. You open the catalog and our conversation begins.

Fall 2003

How fortunate I am to have a desk job that allows me to get out and see things. Where else could an administrator step out of his office and look at a horizon that spreads out to the edge of the world? Where else could a director answer a question about glass furnaces, insurance, or slide presentations and then hear an osprey crying overhead or hear the honk of migrating geese?

When I'm done typing or talking on the phone, I'm one step away from the natural world. In the spring the spruce trees are spreading yellow pollen that gathers in the coves. In the fall the ducks are rafting up and a loon calls out in cooler air. Even inside the office, I can see the world is changing, the islands vanishing in the summer fog or reappearing in brilliant light, rising from the water as if being seen for the first time.

I don't have a bad commute, either. I can walk from the office to my cabin and see the lichen luminescent after a rain, or watch where the sunlight is filtered by the spruce trees whose roots snake out over the granite ledge and boulders.

I like to think of being able to move from the office out into this remarkable world as part of my job description, as if wander is written somewhere in between programming and fundraising or right before other tasks as assigned. It's my way of staying in touch with what's around me and the land and world on which Haystack perches.

Another way I wander is to visit the studios. I can follow the progress of a workshop over the course of a session, from the quiet first moments when people are unsure of each other's names to the final days when it feels like you have always been here and there is nothing else to do but complete the work you started. Each studio has its own working rhythm, its own ways of concentration and relaxation. Some people work early in the morning, others late at night. I'm energized by each visit.

Some days my wandering is curtailed and I have to stay at my desk. This fall during our New England Workshop, Bill Fiorini's students were forging billets of steel, the first step in making Damascus steel. Although that morning I wasn't able to visit the forge, I could hear the blacksmiths at work, each blow of the power hammer traveling on the wind down to the main campus. I felt like it was calling out to me, an auditory manifestation of the creative energy that abounds in the Haystack studios. Unlike the sound, though, which travels in its waves over the water until it is fainter and fainter, the energy of the studios grows greater in its intensity. By the end of a session, it's a pulsating force on the campus. I think of that energy traveling outward from Haystack, those ideas and ways of seeing that didn't exist before you arrived, moving out into the world, where we are all wandering.

Spring 2004

This winter I took a two-month sabbatical break, my first in 15 years. It was a challenge to detach myself from my established routine, but I was excited to leave. My desk was clean and my email was shut off. I wanted to spend time writing, reading, and traveling with my family. I even thought I'd teach myself to juggle four balls. I'm still working on that one. I began my journey in late November in Vermont working on a new manuscript of poems as the first snows began and ice worked its way from the edges to the middle of the rivers. Then our family traveled to Arizona where the ancient oceanic geology reveals itself in a sparse landscape and the horizon is endless. I ended my break in Mexico at the end of January, where my head was overflowing with Spanish words and I was like a child learning that there are names for everything.

On the first morning back at work at the beginning of February, I was reading my e-mails, going through the piles of correspondence and publications, and becoming reacquainted with my job. I felt like someone coming out of anesthesia—everything was moving a little more slowly as bits and pieces of who I was and what I did came back to me. I became a visitor in my own work life—I could watch myself remember what I did.

After spending a day organizing my desk at our winter office in Deer Isle village, I drove to the school, up the icy road to the campus where we have been working during the winter on an expansion of Gateway. As part of our new capital campaign we're adding an exhibition area on the west side of the auditorium.

Standing in the chilly air inside the building, with the chairs pushed to one side amid the chaos of construction, both the building and I were in our winter dormancy. But being in that space I could begin to remember all the people who have gathered here and all the ideas that have been born from the exchanges among them. I was struck by the enormity of its purpose and the modesty of its scale. It's a small space, really, compared to what it can hold—generations of makers from all over and ideas and skills that have traveled centuries and millennia.

That's when the slow motion of my return ended, and I could feel the power of what we do at Haystack. Out of emptiness we create a space where people gather and become a community, a community of making with the silence of creation at its core. I loved standing in the new space and looking from one end to the other. It was like an empty vessel waiting to be filled.

Fall 2004

This fall we began building a new visiting artist's studio. This is the final component of recent renovations that we've undertaken through the Campaign for Haystack: Renovation and Renewal. As part of the campaign we also built a second office module and added an exhibition and storage area to the Gateway auditorium.

Before we could begin the construction of the new studio, though, we had to remove the old one. Many of you are familiar with the building that we've used recently as a workspace for visiting artists, but may not know its history. In the fall and winter of 1960-61 it was the original construction building where the contractor kept the blueprints, and even though it wasn't part of the campus design, it remained and took on various uses after the school was completed. It was moved from its original location between what is now the bell tower and loading dock and became the school store, aptly named "Goods in the Woods" for its location a little removed from the campus. The building expanded in the mid-60s to eventually become our library. After we built a new store and library in 1997, we began to use the space as a studio for visiting artists.

While the building had outlived its usefulness for us, we were sure it had many uses left, and in Maine, a place of practicality and resourcefulness, people don't like to see things go to waste. Those of you who have scavenged at our Deer Isle landfill have seen this tradition of use and reuse in action. Old windows may become part of a greenhouse, couches and lamps can have their lives extended in someone else's home, and a battered gas can and old gears may become elements of a sculpture by a Haystack student.

We asked around to see who might want this worn but sound building and Phil Retberg, a carpenter who is working on the new building, was interested in using it as a workshop and for storage and for housing young livestock on his farm in Penobscot. Because the building was too wide to make it down our road, a crew came and cut it apart between the gable-roofed and shed-roofed sections and braced it with 2x4s. A few days later Phil returned with Paul Brayton, who has a hydraulically operated trailer he uses to move boats, to move the building to its new home across the bridge.

A building on a flat bed takes up a lot of space, particularly on our narrow Haystack road. Paul patiently negotiated the tight curves, backing up and maneuvering slowly forward. At one point the two men built up cribbing under the building and drove the trailer out from under it to reposition it better for the journey. I was inspired by their resourcefulness and ingenuity. There was no owner's manual for something like this; they had to figure it out on the spot.

It's the same kind of figuring out that I see in the studios at Haystack, where we use skills that grow out of intuition, observation, and practice to engage clay, fabric, wood, glass, metal or whatever material speaks to us. What we make evolves from the conversation between hand, idea, and materials. As with any conversation, there's speaking and listening.

It took two trips over a few days for the building to make it to Penobscot, where it sits on a hillside. It's still in two parts, waiting to be joined together to become something else.

Spring 2005

For me the first hint of spring appears toward the end of February. That's when the utility poles alongside Route 15 are decorated with signs bearing the names of the basketball players and cheerleaders from the high school, providing a visual cheer for the teams as they head off the island to compete in state tournaments. The signs, which appear overnight, are surprising blossoms on the poles, our first flowers. While it's not exactly spring, it's a signal—along with the longer daylight—that we've turned a corner. Another sure indication of the winter's departure are the blaze orange signs with bold black letters that say frost heave or bump, alerting us to the deteriorating condition of the road. Sometimes those warnings are attached to utility poles, other times they're hung from trees. The point is to get the message as close to the action as possible. The end of winter is a geology lesson on the impact of freezing and thawing on clay, stone, and soil. It's also an opportunity to learn the value (and sometimes the replacement cost) of a car's shock absorbers and struts.

In its relentless way water alters a landscape. Sometimes this is a process that takes millions of years; in a Maine winter, though, it takes only a few months to transform roads. They rise up with the frost, water drains down through cracks and fissures, and the weight of traffic moves the asphalt around as well. Driving becomes an adventure where, if you forget the location of a particularly big heave, your muffler scrapes the pavement and your coffee jumps out of your travel mug. The worst stretches of the road can make me feel like I'm a downhill skier descending over moguls or that I'm on a new carnival ride at the Blue Hill Fair. I realize that the blacktop is really only an impermanent veneer of civilization over the older story of earth and water.

It's not a good time of year to be in a hurry, particularly on an unfamiliar road. This year I've been thinking that driving in the world of frost heaves can be a kind of meditation, a signal that time is all we have and that every excursion is an opportunity to slow down and remember this. It reminds me of how I feel at the entrance to Haystack in the summer, when we drive up the road that is really granite ledge delineating the ancient contour of the earth.

Both roads are signals to take our time. At the entrance to Haystack it's the perfect message since we're entering a different kind of time. The hours aren't any longer here, but we're seeing them differently. We have the time to pay attention to our work. We have the time to talk with one another. We have the time to watch the tide rise and fall. We have the time to go inside a question and stay there for a while.

Fall 2005

Sitting in the busy Haystack dining hall at mealtime I can find myself entering into interesting discussions. If I'm positioned in the middle of two conversations, I'm sometimes able to float between both. So it was during our New Works retreat session for former faculty that I was moving in and out of topics that included poetry, the uses of profanity, t-shirts with slogans, drilled and dug wells, mathematical puzzles, wood heat, and the potential energy of one day of sunlight.

I like the juxtaposition of these disparate worlds; perhaps it makes for a starting place for art if I combine two unlikely subjects in my brain, like poetry and well drilling, and soon I'm somewhere in the world of metaphorical aquifers and healing waters. It's a way of jump-starting my own mind—where I can become a little lost and things get stranger, in a good way.

I particularly appreciate the range of topics that come up when I'm sitting with people who work in craft media; sooner or later the topic will turn to how things are made. There is a deepness to makers' understanding of wood or clay or metal—how the material moves and how they can interact with it. That in itself is a kind of conversation—a dialogue—in every act of making. At the same time it's a practical view of the world, one that respects age-old ways of working and appreciates the importance of a good tool.

Another conversation you might hear at a Haystack table is one that makes distinctions between art and craft. This isn't a conversation that I want to enter into right now, but if there is one thing that distinguishes people who work with craft materials, it's the way that they can figure things out, with their hands, and solve problems.

Being able to solve problems in a practical and sometimes elegant way, and to know a material well enough to anticipate how it will respond, are attributes that one would wish for all the leaders of the world. Implicit in this is an ingenuity that is aware of limitations. And this ingenious way of working can be metaphorical and useful all at the same time, like a beautiful cup that you hold in your hands and raise toward your lips.

Spring 2006

Haystack is a thrilling place for me when our studios are full of creative people working day and night. It's like a country with a different sense of time and the only occupations are making and discovery.

When the school is in session, though, my own time is divided differently, so I don't have the opportunity to investigate ideas in an uninterrupted way. Fortunately for me, I occasionally can take the time in the winter to go away to write—to have my own "Haystack" in another place. In December I went to the Vermont Studio Center for two weeks, where I joined a community of about 50 writers and visual artists. There's no ocean to contemplate, but I could watch ice form on the Gihon River, changing each day with the temperature, leaving a record of its flow.

There I was, able to spend days and nights writing. What a luxury to spend an entire morning contemplating and refining imagery. As always, there are moments when I feel that I am able to say things I've never said before and other times where my voice sounds predictable, like a tape looping over and over again. The truth is always somewhere in between and staying with the work helps sort that out.

During my time at the Studio Center, there was a discussion about art making and meditation practice—a talk among some of the residents about the impact of one practice on the other. As we began the discussion, there was for me an inference that in meditation there is no past or future, only now. I must confess to feeling claustrophobic, as if I would be trapped in a world with no entry or exit, no memories or aspirations.

At that moment, I happened to look at my half-filled journal on the table in front of me. Reflecting on the present, on now, I realized that half of my journal was filled—with words and experiences. Inside it were the places I've been and the people I love, so there was a past; I could see it tangibly. In the other half of my journal were the blank white pages of my future, the unknown and unwritten. I didn't want to give up either of these, past or future, and it wasn't that they didn't exist, but that the moment to enter into fully was this one, now.

When people are at work in the Haystack studios it's the same way. We are informed by who we have been, and the material we are working with also has its own memory and legacy— of how it behaves, and of the heritage of makers who have used it over sometimes thousands of years. But the moment we put our hands on it, we are in a new world of now. And if we are present, we can find ourselves paying attention in a different way, we can find ourselves listening attentively to the material, and hearing clearly as if for the first time.

Fall 2006

Priscilla Merritt passed away at ninety-three, on the last day of our final session of the summer. Pris, wife of Haystack's founding director Francis Merritt (1913-2000), had been involved in the life of the school since she and Fran were hired as co-directors and had traveled from Flint, Michigan to Haystack's first home in Montville, Maine back in 1951. Pris was there at the beginning and remained active in the school's activities until her death. She was the first weaving instructor, and then, when the school needed a cook (the person who had been hired was unable to take the job) she ably took over that role. Pris had never cooked for a group that large, but in the spirit of improvisation that is at the heart of the school, she figured it out. Bill Brown, assistant director at the time, advised her that all she had to do was multiply.

Both those early roles were appropriate ones for her—not just in a practical way, but also in a metaphorical way. The structure of the school—the warm on which we still weave today, was due in part to her, in the graciousness and civility that both she and Fran brought to Haystack, in their belief in the value of sharing information freely and mixing tradition and innovation. Her vision for a cuisine that complements the school's creative life is still with us; that we are nurtured and sustained by our common meals goes beyond the abundant food on our plates.

After the school moved to Deer Isle in 1961, Pris opened a gallery, Centennial House. At a time when there were very few galleries exhibiting contemporary craft, Pris showed the work of leading makers of the day—Karen Karnes, Toshiko Takaezu, Dale Chihuly and others, and she welcomed students and faculty to receptions at her home every session.

She also had an exceptional memory, and could recount in great detail the early work of the Board of Directors and Mary Beasom Bishop, our founder. She would remember fondly students from the 50s, 60s, and 70s whose names are now so well recognized in the field, and keep track of the lives of hundreds of former students and teachers.

Pris served as an honorary trustee, and we would talk regularly about new programs and initiatives. Last winter we were having a conversation and she said, "Dear, you're doing things that we never dreamed of." It didn't take long for me to respond, "We wouldn't be able to do the things we're doing now if you hadn't dreamed what you dreamed." It was an intuitive response on my part, because one dream is always built on another, just as one story is built on another, and wherever we stand today it is because others were here before us. This is what makes craft compelling to us, because in the very materials there is a history and a life, and when we roll up our sleeves and get to work, we are both the ones who are making change and are ourselves changed at the same time.

Spring 2007

Last spring my wife Susan and I purchased a house on Deer Isle. It's an old boarding house—once called the Pleasant View Hotel—that had been gutted and not lived in year-round for many years. Owning an older home with no furnace and minimal plumbing is a great way to learn about heating systems and be thankful for the blessings of running water. This is our work in progress—a project that will keep us busy for a while. Working on a house is like working with art materials—there is a give and take, conversations between you and the old walls, floor joists, foundation stones, and rattling windows. And, like making art, you can uncover challenges that don't lend themselves to ready-made solutions.

In the fall, we realized that we needed to improve the drainage around the 150-year-old foundation. We worked with Rick Weed, a heavy equipment operator with an incredibly light touch with an excavator, and Dan Foss, a carpenter and mason who has repaired and nursed many old structures. Rick dug out a ten-foot section of the foundation wall on the uphill side of the house, revealing the large glacial boulders that support many of the old buildings on the Island. He had expected to find mortar between the stones, which could then be re-pointed. After that, he would set a perforated drainpipe near the surface. There was no mortar, though, only loose dirt, and nothing but compression holding things in place. If Dan attempted to clean the wall to patch it, he would knock down many of the smaller rocks, leaving the foundation in worse shape than when we began.

With our first solution gone, Dan, Rick, Susan, and I stood looking at the empty space. At this point, some people might have begun suggesting the answers right away, just to hear their own voices. Perhaps because this is Maine, or perhaps because these men were used to moving big and heavy objects, they had a different sense of pacing. The first thing they did was to contemplate the problem. No one said anything. They spent a while taking it in, at least a few minutes in silence. Next, Rick asked Dan what he thought. More silence. Finally, Dan said he thought we should leave the wall undisturbed and put crushed stone against it, allowing the water to drain away more easily. "We've all lived long enough," Dan said, "to realize that not everything is perfect, but it can work." Rick agreed with this new approach and continued excavating the remainder of the foundation, gracefully maneuvering the big bucket within a foot of the house.

I appreciated at the moment that both of them understood materials, and they both realized that they were solving a problem, not trying to out-do each other with solutions. They were listening to the house, in a way, and doing what made the most sense. These two men brought the same things to working on our foundation that craft makers bring to their work: knowledge based on experience and humility in working with the earth. I see this often at Haystack—makers who call on creativity that reaches back to the first hands. Humans working with materials are ingenious at solving problems, and this ingenuity is what unites us—scientists, chefs, potters, and plumbers—and allows us to see not what we expected, but what is, and make the best of it.

Fall 2007

Charlie Gailis, longtime Haystack trustee who passed away in the Fall of 2005, had long ago provided for Haystack in his will, designating the money for scholarships and innovative programs. But that fall, Mary Nyburg, also a Haystack trustee and owner of the Blue Heron Gallery, was selling her home and adjacent barn. Like many of us at the school, Charlie envisioned this as a perfect place for Haystack to have its year-round offices and to also establish an exhibition and workshop space for the community. He decided to allocate part of the proceeds of his estate to doing this.

Charlie knew that he only had a few months to live, and there was an urgency to his actions in making sure his estate was in order. He could also witness the impact of his generosity—we were able to agree to buy the house and begin to plan renovations before he died that December.

Haystack also wanted to recognize Charlie's incredible generosity by commissioning artwork that would be in his memory. I spoke with him about asking Eddie Dominguez, who had completed three other mural projects on the island, to create a mosaic mural at the new center in Charlie's memory. Charlie was touched by the idea, and asked that we have people who knew him contribute to the content in some way.

This fall Eddie came to Haystack to begin work on the mosaic, using our new visiting artist's studio as his working space. Earlier, to honor Charlie's request, we had asked people close to him to share their memories of him, and Eddie began work to incorporate their sentiments into the piece. The emotional consensus was that Charlie was a man who worked behind the scenes, and didn't call attention to himself. Eddie began to work with this in mind, and at the same time was taken with the large boulders, the glacial erratics, that stand nearby the studio, and the way that the spruce trees grew around and against them, and the ferns, lichen and moss covered the tops.

It happened that at the same time that Eddie was working on the piece, we held our biannual New Works workshop—a five-day retreat where former faculty can work in any studio to develop new ideas for work. Eddie invited people to help him, and many came by and placed the tile shards to help create the image. One of the participants who was eager to contribute was Winnie Owens-Hart. Winnie had first come to Haystack as a scholarship student because of Charlie. According to Winnie, he had "convinced her to come and have an experience..." and she did, studying with the Nigerian potter Abbas Awuhan. As she puts it, "This experience touched all my senses." As a direct result she went on to study in Africa and change the character of her work. Winnie helped Eddie one evening, talking about Charlie as they worked, years away from her first studio time at Haystack, yet still connected to that moment.

This seemed to me the most fitting, and touching, contribution, from someone who knew Charlie, and it was one that we hadn't anticipated. Here were art and spirit coming together—a manifestation of how our lives intersect and we shape one another. We don't always know where we are going. We make plans and things happen. It's a kind of dance, whether we are managing our own lives or managing an organization. It happens when we are making art, going on a journey, or repairing the world. The expected and the unexpected converge. That's the moment to wait for.

Spring 2008

By the time you get this in the mail, lilacs or forsythia may be blossoming. There might be a light spring rain when you can smell the earth. Black flies could be out, too, swarming around your head. I began writing, though, after I had just experienced a morning in northern Vermont when it was twenty-two degrees below zero (Fahrenheit). Then the following day I drove back to Deer Isle through a heavy, wet snow, where it was at times hard to tell the road from the shoulder. A drive like that can feel even longer than it is—at 40 miles per hour it was pretty long to begin with—and it feels like all that exists in the world is me in the little capsule of my car, floating in the white-out world of hyperspace. It's a journey that focuses me on the task at hand and Nature's power.

Weather is our here and now. We love to talk about it. Often I will receive emails that begin or end with what the weather is like at the sender's home, and I can respond with a weather report of my own. I can share the details of it at the hardware store or post office. I certainly enjoyed telling people about my twenty-two below morning. In a world that exists increasingly outside the physical, weather is something that touches all of us everyday. We look forward to it, or complain about it, or we expect that it should behave just the way the National Weather Service says it will. And those days that are forecast and arrive, those days of rain and sleet, fog, or clear blue sky, are the days we all share. Wherever we are, they make us into a community, since we are all in it together.

At Haystack, when we are perched on the granite ledge at the edge of the sea, we are certainly aware of the weather. Sometimes we say that the kitchen is the seventh studio; then weather must be the eighth studio. We come to know it and are influenced by its changes. There are the foggy days when the moisture condenses on the tips of the spruce needles and curls the photocopy paper. There are the dry spells when the moss cracks and there are moments after a rain when the lichen on the trees is luminescent. There are the clear, full-moon-nights when the moon is enormous on the horizon and the light makes a path right to our shore.

Sometimes at our orientation on the first night of a session, I will make a point of telling people that there is not good weather or bad weather, there is only weather, and we can experience it together. It reminds me of how we work with the materials of craft—when our expectations and hands meet the tangible stuff of the earth—and it isn't a matter of enforcing our will on something, but of listening and responding. It's a good way to be alive in the world.

Haystack is a place that is full of sounds. Day and night, from the hammer shaping steel on the anvil, to the saw cutting through the growth lines of a board, to the shuttle joining warp and weft to make a fabric, to the roar of the furnaces as glass and clay are transformed, there seems always to be the sound of materials becoming something else as our ideas meet them. There are even the sounds we make when we are not working in the studios, like the many conversations in the dining room, the laughter of new friendships filling the space, or just the general rustle and excitement when dessert is brought out, the sweet break in a long day.

There are also sounds that feel almost like silences—the water lapping against the granite, the ospreys crying high overhead, or the wind in the tops of the spruce trees.

And, of course, there is no gathering of makers where there isn't the sound of people discussing ideas about making, from the intent implicit in the work to the hierarchies of the various art forms. We're interested not only in how we make work, but how we describe that work as well. In recognition of this, in July we held a conference, The Language of Craft, that investigated how we talk and write about craft objects and craft making. We discussed the language that we use to describe our work and the creative process, critical writing about craft, and the role that language plays in the creation of work—and how this influences our work and our perceptions of the field.

Because of Haystack's scale, our conferences allow us not only to have lectures, but to have studio-based activities as well. We think this is a great complement to discussion, because it gives us the opportunity to have our hands contemplate the same ideas that our voices have been working on.

Even though the conference was about language, or perhaps because of this, we decided to have one of the art-making activities in silence. We structured the activity so that each person was randomly given one of about ten words to respond to—words like expand, fragile, crumple—and we had to work without speaking, with only minimal materials—paper, string, tape, and wire—and create something that responded to that word.

We worked in silence for about forty-five minutes, seventy people working on the decks or in the studios and reconvened to see what we had made. These obviously weren't finished pieces, but it was remarkable to see what had grown out of that brief interlude of silence, work that the makers may find contains within it many more ideas. It was a reminder to us all, too, that before language begins and before making begins, there is always the silence of getting started. It's a silence that's good to listen to.

The economy has been on everyone's mind. It has even taken the place of the weather as a favorite topic of conversation. Since the fall—or perhaps I should say autumn so as not to confuse a season with plummeting financial markets—we can discuss the subtleties of credit and investments and wake up at night wondering where it will all lead. We might yearn for the simpler days when makers could barter their wares, trading pottery for food.

The directness and simplicity of this idea is compelling and hearkens back to our earliest days as makers, but wherever we live, we are most certainly touched by systems that are beyond our control. And in this new turbulent world I am aware of the many issues that affect Haystack and its ability to offer the dynamic and innovative programs for which it is known. To figure things out we use common sense and intuition. We stay alert to our surroundings and the world around us. We talk to people. And, we look to the future with a vision that honors craft at the same time it reinterprets the role of creativity and making.

With our vision comes practicality. We budget carefully and we spend what we take in. Those readers of newsletters of non-profit organizations know that places like Haystack depend on individual donors to make the gifts that make the programming possible. Perhaps because we are rooted in the work of the hand, we take a decidedly hands-on approach to asking for money. In November, when we send out the letter I've written to our alumni and supporters, I sign personalized ones to everyone who has made a contribution in the past ten years, and I look at the names of each of you who have given to the school. I often reflect on the workshop you took, or the workshop you taught, and the community that flourished while you were here. When your contributions come in, sometimes with eloquent notes about the impact that Haystack has had on your life and work, I write another letter, this one thanking you.

In this year, with all of us more aware than ever of the fragility of our economic lives, this exchange of letters and contributions feels to me like holding hands. Your hand touches the letter and the envelope. And even if your contribution is made on-line, I still hold the record of your gift in my hand. Signing each of these many thank you letters I am reminded that every person who makes this investment is supporting the future, and supporting it with optimism and hope. And, like all true gifts, these donations are given freely, out of a spirit of generosity, the same generosity that I see in the teaching and learning in our workshops. This generosity goes beyond supporting Haystack's financial well being; it's the lifeblood of our endeavor.

Fall 2009

Deadlines can be our friends. How else would we get our tax returns and grant proposals completed? How else would we get pedestals painted and artwork framed if it weren't for an exhibition opening? A deadline has a way of sharpening our instincts and helping us to focus on the work at hand. That's the way I've always felt about helping to make Haystack's entry for the Deer Isle Fourth of July Parade. A beautiful float, completed a day late, would travel down an empty road.

The Island parade is a wonderful manifestation of small town life in America. It features, among other things, handmade floats, costumed walkers, fire engines, antique cars, horseback riders, and a rock band or two on flat bed trailers—over fifty entries. The parade makes its way through the center of town, and then turns around at the old elementary school and heads back again—I think because it's worth appreciating twice. The streets are lined with year-round Islanders, summer residents, and tourists, an estimated audience of a few thousand altogether. Usually the parade has a theme about the Island, or history, or cultural heritage. Having a theme makes a framework within which to work; I think of it as the deadline's partner. This year, however, the parade committee chose the non-theme of "anything goes," which left us scratching our heads for a while.

While we didn't have the theme, we still had the deadline,

and had to get to work. I remembered that our summer assistants, Stephen Kent and Lindsay Mis, both had unusual talents—Stephen played the bagpipes and Lindsay could create hats and animals from balloons. If anything goes, certainly bagpipes and balloons would be a start. The weather provided some inspiration too; June was the rainiest month on record in the Northeast—rain and more rain with fog or clouds in between. With this in mind, we began to create a rain dance marching band, where we would wear balloon hats and ponchos made of green garbage bags, carry multi-colored umbrellas, and hold signs with the icons of the forecast—all rain and lightning. Ellen Wieske, our assistant director, created a rain cloud (filled with a hundred helium balloons) that floated over our heads, and Gene Koch, our facilities manager, made drums out of 5 gallon buckets, tin cans, and small raised copper vessels. We were set to march—an entourage of about twenty-five Haystack staff, family members, and students—including ones from Canada, England, Denmark, and Japan experiencing their first American Fourth.

The morning of the parade was foggy, with a feeling of imminent rain, the legacy of the wet June continuing. We quickly improvised our routine—the bagpipes alternating between two songs—"Rain, Rain Go Away" and "You Are My

Sunshine"—the bucket drums making syncopated rhythms. We were joyous marchers, chanting for the rain to go away, dancing and juggling our way along the mile-long route. By the end of the parade it appeared that our anti-rain dance had worked. In what seemed like the first time in weeks, the sky cleared and the sun appeared. Elsewhere along the Eastern seaboard and among meteorologists there may have been other explanations, but for many in the parade crowd, our dancing was credited for the miracle. All that it took was an odd assortment of regular materials, some helium, a little ingenuity, and a beat that you can dance to. For a brief moment the world was transformed, as were we.

Spring 2010

I was very fortunate late this winter to visit Adelaide, South Australia at the invitation of potter Stephen Bowers, managing director of the JamFactory, an innovative craft and design center there. My wife, Susan Webster accompanied me and we had the opportunity to meet with many artists and educators to talk about Haystack and its programs and to learn about institutions in Australia as well. That our visit coincided with the start of the Adelaide Festival, an internationally renowned biennial art event, was an added bonus. There were hundreds of performances, a Fringe Festival, a Writers' Week, and visual arts exhibitions, all featuring international rosters of artists.

Of course it's presumptuous to make judgments about a country or city after only a two-week visit, but it felt like an art heaven to us. There is significant national, state, and municipal support for the arts and lots of vitamin D from the summer sun. Our cultural immersion also included sampling Vegemite—an Australian yeast paste—on toast, having a prawn barbeque, and hearing a sound check by AC/DC, who was performing at the Adelaide Oval—the cricket stadium in town. We didn't know that it was the famous Australian rockers' decibels that were rattling the air, until we asked someone wearing a black t-shirt who was sitting on a park bench. We noticed his shirt said AC/DC, and after that we began seeing that the street was full of black t-shirt wearing men and women of all ages, a secret society of 43,000 rockers who attended the concert. Perhaps that's the way travel is—if your eyes are open you can see a new world in every moment.

One of the most moving works that we saw was in the Adelaide Biennial of Australian Arts—a 10 foot by 20 foot painting by twelve Aboriginal artists—the Martumili Artists—who live in the Punmu community in Western Australia. The painting, Ngartyarta Kujarra (Lake Dora), is a map that depicts a vast salt lake, and includes the surrounding fresh water sources—water that was essential to survival during the time of living nomadically.

We attended a meet-the-artists session and learned that the painting had been done over a one-week period, with all of the women, watched by other members of the community, working outside in temperatures over 100 degrees Fahrenheit. Their vision was to make a painting about their community and to have the sale of the piece support it as well. They would sing while they worked, telling the stories and locations of the waterholes.

At the session someone from the audience asked why they sang. A young Aboriginal woman, who was not one of the painters, but who had assisted with the project, said simply that these were the songlines, and that the women sang about the place so that they knew what they were painting. At the opening of the exhibition the day before, the women had also spontaneously danced the same story that they had sung and painted.

To the Martumili Artists the painting was a map, a history, and a deep connection to place. While this connection is one of the most profound that I have ever witnessed, I think that we all have a connection to ancestors and to place when we are being creative. Certainly the Haystack landscape of granite, spruce, islands, sea, and sky has an impact on anyone working in the studios. But even beyond that, we all carry significant places and stories with us, the places where we started and those we have journeyed to—the places that have shaped us and how we see the world—and we can listen to their songs as we work.

—— *Fall 2010* ————————————

Haystack is in a place of remarkable beauty. The horizon stretches before us, so that every morning, or every clear morning at least, the world appears, as if it had been newly created. And even on those dense foggy mornings when we can't see the horizon, we can feel the dampness on our skin, and know that the living, breathing world is right next to us.

We sometimes can see remarkable natural sights, the kinds that take our breath away. Like those evenings when the full moon rises and the reflected light lets us see so deeply into the dark, past the islands to a mysterious horizon. If we are lucky, in the afternoon, we might see a bald eagle flying over the deck, gliding by quickly, and we feel the thrill of discovery and the visceral connection—that we are joined to something so wild in this moment. Penobscot Bay can bring discoveries too, like seals or dolphins rising to the surface of the bay. And in the evenings we may see the water alive with phosphorescence.

There are less dramatic things to witness also—the small spruce seedlings rising up on the granite ledge, the barnacles and periwinkles feeding in the tide pools, the seeds of the fireweed riding on the wind.

Occasionally we may have a tendency to create a hierarchy of the beauty that we have witnessed, as if seeing an eagle has greater importance than seeing the pollen floating away from the small brown flowers of the spruce trees. Sometimes in our own excitement, we tell someone what they missed if they didn't see the particular phenomenon that we saw, like a night of meteor showers or a rainbow—as if it's a scorecard of natural wonders.

I think the better way to look at it is to realize that, while we might not have been there to see the one wonder, we may have witnessed another. The only time we really miss something is if we are not paying attention. It's not just looking for the biggest wonder, but seeing the world around us with wonder, the shades of green of the moss and lichen after the rain, the monarch butterfly floating down in it's fall migration. Large or small, it's how we're looking, not what we're looking at, and if we are paying attention, then the world can be alive in every moment.

By now you've probably read the 2011 Haystack catalog and imagined yourself in a studio, remembered a workshop you took, or made plans to be here this summer. I'm glad that you were able to hold it in your hands. There were a few days in January when we were worried that the catalog, filled with all those creative possibilities, might not make it into the mail.

This problem arose because we've changed the way that we do our bulk mailings, and instead of sending the catalog from Maine, it's mailed from a large postal center near where it's printed, in Virginia. When an official there looked up the school's name in the postal service's national database, we were listed as Haystack Mountain School—'of Crafts' hadn't made it in. Our catalog return address had our full name, and since this didn't match exactly with the name in the database, the by-the-book official wasn't going to approve our mailing paperwork, and the catalogs wouldn't be mailed. Working through our friendly local post office—where mail addressed only "Haystack School Maine" might get delivered—we were able to access the national database and straighten things out.

While we were in the middle of this confusion (theirs, not ours) about our name, the words "common sense" came to mind. What was the concern here? Were there two competing institutions in Deer Isle, Maine—one focused on rappelling down cliff faces and the other on working with our hands and materials—and this was part of an elaborate deception to attract students to another program? Our complex world needs complex safeguards, but we forget sometimes how simple things can be. In this case, I assume that many years ago, someone filling out a form by hand couldn't fit our long name in the space.

When I confront situations like this, I sometimes tell the person on the other end of the phone a story about Neil Armstrong, the first man on the moon. When he was landing the lunar module he wisely overrode the computer, which had selected a boulder-strewn site, and landed the spacecraft on his own. It's the human intervention that's compelling. And what a complex moment that was. Landing where no one had gone before, and needing to make a judgment, a man used his hands to make the right choice.

We face these choices all the time. It's not an either or situation. It's knowing the appropriate way to respond. When we talk about the hand, much more than our remarkable sense of touch is involved. We are really talking about human intervention and imagination; grasping a situation and understanding the feel and the weight of it. It is always a balancing act, where the rules can give us the form, and our senses can give us the spirit. The wisdom is in that balance.

After our programs at the campus are finished in mid-October, Haystack takes on a much quieter personality. Our stalwart maintenance and technical staff—Gene Koch, Kit Loekle, and Jonathan Doolan—can work around the campus with hardly an interruption. No one is lined up to eat in the dining room, and at night it's a much darker world with no lights on in the studios. The rope for the bell tower sways in the wind, but it's not calling anybody to meals or presentations. The crows caw to one another and the red squirrels get ready for winter.

What we are left with when everyone is gone are the spruce decks and cedar shingled buildings and the world that was here before the campus was built—spruce and fir trees, granite ledge, moss and lichen—telling an older story.

The fall and winter are also a time when we can work on larger facility projects, and in October our contractor, Walter Kumiega from Cedar Lane Construction, began the replacement of the walkway on our lower tier of cabins. This entails ripping out all of the decking and joists and replacing some of the concrete piers that support it as well.

I went to check on the progress of the construction last week, but arrived after the work crew had gone. I walked down the stairs alongside the dorm bathrooms and when I got to the bottom, the stairway was unattached and the walkway wasn't there. The cabins stood on either side, but with only space between them, space and the forest floor—the dark soil, the granite ledge, small boulders. The ground was muddy that day, and it felt as if the glaciers that shaped this part of the coast hadn't been gone that long.

What was most surprising to me with the walkway gone was seeing what a light footprint Haystack has. Take away a deck and you would hardly know anyone had been here. I've only known this particular landscape with our buildings on it, but seeing the empty space I could imagine that time when the straight grid of the campus was being laid out, and architect Edward Larrabee Barnes' idea began to take physical shape, a brilliant design that over time has created an intuitive harmony with its surroundings.

While there is very little that makes up this campus—a little concrete and wooden framing, roofs that keep us mostly dry—it's that very simplicity that makes it all the more remarkable. In a world where better is all too often defined as bigger and possibly speedier too, the buildings themselves, and the discoveries that take place day and night inside the studios—are manifestations of a different way to look at things. Perhaps it's taking what is most essential, and examining it as creatively and deeply as we can. We may realize we don't need as much as we thought we did after all.

Public Talks

Rochester Institute of Technology, 2002
Glass Art Society, 2003
William Jamison Lecture, Oregon, 2005

If You Can't Find Inspiration at First,
Give Yourself a Deadline:
Some Thoughts on the Creative Process

Rochester Institute of Technology, 2002

I begin to get ready to write this for you. The late afternoon
mid-March sunlight has grown stronger; it fills the south-facing
rooms in the house. I make a cup of tea. I watch the sunlight.
I turn on the radio. I play solitaire. Aretha Franklin is on the
radio singing "Dark End of the Street," the kind of music that
can evoke deep emotions. Even if I'm not sure what the emotions are, I know that some emotional current is circulating,
connecting me to the radio. A song is like a hymn and a hymn
is like a prayer and every creative act is a kind of prayer or hope.
I see the sunlight through the crack of the door into my room.
I've been thinking all day about writing for you. When I awoke,
when I went out for a run, when I went for a walk. Then there
was a big step. I turn the computer on and get to work. One
word follows another in the afternoon. I'm off and running. I'll
be through this again and again, I'll print this text out, I'll scribble notes in the margins, I'll re-write. I'll scribble some more. I
continue to procrastinate. I think of calling a friend. I want to
make another cup of tea.

Perhaps getting started is the hardest part. I could compare
writing to swimming in the ocean in Downeast Maine. It's as
much a baptism as a swim. In the summer months, even on
a warm day, the water numbs my body as I prepare to enter.
Numb to the ankles and then numb to the waist. Finally taking

the plunge into the water, cold water numbing my chest, taking my breath away, but I'm in the ocean. My breathing regulates, white cumulus clouds float in the sky. I float on the water. The ocean lifts me.

* * * *

Our species has been making things for a long time. Last month I read in the New York Times about an archeological dig in the southern tip of Africa. Dr. Christian Henshilwood of the South African Museum in Cape Town found "finely polished weapon points" that were made 70,000 years ago.

"Why so finely polished?" Dr Henshilwood asked. "It's actually unnecessary for projectile points to be so carefully made. It suggests to us that this is an expression of symbolic thinking. The people said, 'Let's make a beautiful object'." (New York Times February 26, 2002 "Archeological Relics Fuel Debate on When Humans Became Human.")

From 70,000 years ago until now we've created a lot of things. We've built shelters, made storage vessels, adorned our bodies, woven our clothes, domesticated plants and animals, and harnessed the energy of the win and the sun. Everything we see around us we've touched in some way. Everything travels with its own genealogy. And now I'm using words that have evolved from ancient languages over thousands of years, the computer plugged into wires in the wall that go to a pole in the street that connects to a grid that electrifies the whole country. Anything that I'm doing is built on something done by someone before me. When I was a potter many years ago, I was attracted to the sense of timeless time and intimate history of the hands that had formed the vessels, reaching back into our ancient past.

So when we begin to create we are supported by discoveries and ideas that surround us and inform what we do. As a culture we are not much given to venerating the past, but we've come from somewhere and behind us is a remarkable and flawed progression of human history that carries us right up to this moment. At the same time, we're on our own, and every entry into the world of making is a whole new start.

I thought the best way to give you my thoughts on the creative process would be to take you through the processes that I use to write. My own history as a maker goes back to the first poem I wrote in 5th grade. Our teacher, Mrs. Carrigan, asked us to write a poem. Poetry wasn't one of our regular writing assignments. As I think back on it, it felt like a special day. There was no particular topic given. For some reason, maybe hunger, I decided to write about food. The first line came to me right away: "There are many things in the world to eat." That certainly gave me a lot of possibilities. The poem included bananas, bacon, and beets, with beets rhyming with eat. I raided a refrigerator and grew as big as an alligator. Somewhere during the life of the poem that afternoon, Mrs. Carrigan took artistic control—she altered the rhythm, and added some adult expressions. I don't think my teacher helped me solve problems so much as solve them for me—not the best model for the creative process. Still, when I was finished I knew I had made something that hadn't existed before. I felt that something had grown inside of me.

That same year I was driving with my parents on the Garden State Parkway, I think near the Dutch Boy Paint sign, a billboard with the Dutch Boy perched with his paint brush and a clock in the corner, south bound traffic headed for the Jersey Shore. I said that the air smelled like Vaseline, probably not an unusual occurrence in that area of the state. "You should write that down," my father said, "that what writers do, they observe things." I guess you could say that by the end of the 5th grade I had understood two important elements of the creative process—discovery and observation.

In my own writing I move back and forth between what is and what if. We know the world around us, our families, our friends, the way the sunlight falls on a building, the way we make coffee in the morning. We know the rituals of our lives. Sometimes just looking at what you know, looking deeply, can take you to another place. For me I try to start with something that I know in a particular way. I want to combine the intimate with the mundane, like describing the inside of my car.

Starting the Subaru at Five Below

After six Maine winters and 100,000 miles
when I take it to be inspected

I search for gas stations where they
just say beep the horn and don't ask me to
put it on the lift, exposing its soft
rusted underbelly. Inside is the record

of commuting: apple cores, a bag from
McDonald's, crushed Dunkin' Donuts cups,

a flashlight that doesn't work and one
that does, gas receipts blurred beyond

recognition. Fingertips numb, nose
hair frozen, I pump the accelerator

and turn the key. The battery cranks,
the engine gives 2 or 3 low groans and

starts. My God it starts. And unlike
my family in the house, the job I'm

headed towards, the poems in my briefcase,
the dreams I had last night, there is

no question about what makes sense.
White exhaust billowing from the tail pipe,

heater blowing, this car is going to
move me, it's going to take me places.

The raw materials are the things I know well. What happens in a poem or any work of art is that we're taking the raw materials—the what is—and transforming it. I don't want my process to replicate what exists. If that were the case, I could have just gone to my car and looked around. I want the act of writing to show me something I don't know; I want the subject to be transformed. How big the transformation is depends on the architecture of the piece itself. For me it's the ordering of the material—the setting of the scene—and the near miracle of the car starting.

At the other end of my writing is a world of "what if," which extends the raw material of words into the world of imagination. For a long time my eyes have taken in the houses in our rural landscape, many 19th century Greek Revival capes, with a stark and beautiful presence in our boulder strewn landscape of fields and spruce woods. At the same time I was thinking about how we use the phrase "house of" in expressions—house of cards, house of pizza, house of prayer, house of horrors. I began to envision the houses near me in a different way; I imagined other lives inside them.

House of Thanksgiving

In the house of thanksgiving
I have seen the angels late at night,
the incandescent light still on downstairs.
They are writing psalms with quills

they pull from their wings.
They toss crumpled drafts into the wood stove
and smoke rises from the chimney,
still holding the shape of the words

then feathers out into a gray landscape.
The soot makes a film on the shrubs.
These angels sing their songs of praise
until they have moved past irony

into full-on love, and kiss one another
with passion, and become like children

at a family gathering,
running from room to joyous room

in the circle of downstairs.
If I watch them all night, at dawn
I see the birch branches shaking in lavender light
like fine capillaries where this world flows into the next

and if I step outside my own house
I can hear them laughing
and hear the heavy thud
of their footsteps in prayer.

I think every creative act combines what we know and what we don't know. If we know where we are going when we set out in the process of making, we end up with something that's of no interest to ourselves. And if it's of no interest to us, it's not likely that it will be of interest to our viewers or readers either.

My own preference is for the work that is a little out of control than for the one that's too controlled. I'd rather see the journey in the discovery, where someone made a synthesis that didn't exist before. I'm not talking about always-large moments either. A poem can be a small moment, each cup or bowl we make can be a small moment, but within those moments we can travel great distances.

Transformation isn't always easy. If it were, and if I were more disciplined, I'd have a poem everyday. We can have the skills to produce something and we can have the material, but sometimes our skills and our material have to simmer, just the way that water and vegetables don't make soup right away. One thing needs to blend into another. The unspoken extra ingredient is time. I need time to reflect on, to recollect, an experience. I think I know what I need to say, yet as soon as I've said it, it's not what I thought it was. I need time and I need to not have expectations about what it is I've written.

I used to go fly-fishing with some friends of mine on a pond in Northern Maine. I wasn't much of a fisherman, but I did manage on my first trip to catch a fish the first time out in the boat. I didn't expect to write anything about that, but the experience, the time on the pond in a canoe, waiting, knowing that there was something mysterious below the surface, registered in some way. A few years later, I was at the ocean, and the rhythm of the tides was present for me everyday. Then, in a time of spiritual questioning, I was able to call on these images. The images had resided in my memory long enough that I could call on them in a natural way to express something else.

I Am Fishing for God

using my heart as bait.
It is just before dawn,
the slightest hint of

pink bleeds into the
night sky. I use my
pen knife to cut the

hole in my chest,
reaching behind the
pocket of my shirt.

What a tough muscle
to pull the hook through.
The heart is astonished

to be in this other world
and trembles and shivers like
a moth discovered in daylight.

I try to calm it by stroking it
by telling it that it will all be
ok, but what do I know.

The breeze picks up and chills the cavern
in my chest. It feels good to
be empty at last. I cast my heart

across the water. I cast it again
and again. Sometimes it floats on
the surface, other times it sinks

below. Something will strike at it
that I can't see. I pray
I am using the right bait.

The rough outer layers
soften in the water. The heart grows
smaller, more pliant.

It has become a beautiful
blue jewel. I begin
not to recognize it.

Was this me?
It waits, I wait.
The boat rocks

slightly in the breeze
lifted and lowered
by the tide.

I had held on to some of these images for a few years, but had
not found the opportunity to use them. But when there came
a moment—the catalyst was a time of questioning in my life—
when there was a deep internal need to say something, then the
images that I had stored with me could be put to service. The
central image in the poem came to me as I woke from a dream.

There are many ways we can be creative. We can be creative when we cook and when we make up excuses. We can
be creative when we repair a car, build a house, make a meal,
or travel to another country. I am in awe of the ways in which
our species has taught itself to survive. And in any skill we have
learned, there are countless adaptations and modifications;
small moments when we make just the right decision to make
something succeed. The nuances and skills that carpenters or
plumbers bring to every project are a kind of creativity, a doctor
treating a patient is a kind of creativity.

Creativity and knowledge go hand in hand. We understand the material and then we can interpret it. Somewhere

along the way in our culture, we separated the sacred from the creative. What attracts people to the creative work of the arts is that there is an implied holiness to what it does. We are attracted to viewing and making because it sets moments aside; it slows down time for us, and allows us to reflect on our relationship to ourselves and the world that surrounds us. I'd like to think of all of our occupations as a continuum of creativity, making a dwelling, making a meal, making a poem, can all be joined together in some way. When we are creating a work of art we're also looking for, and hoping to provide, inspiration. Inspiration, with its Latin root in spirare, to breathe, and we're hoping to breathe new life into the work, into ourselves and into our audience as well.

I've described a few ways that I may work in developing a piece, from observation, memory, and imagining. Sometimes I'm poised and ready to work and excited to get at the task. But there are other times when I don't feel, at least on the surface, that there's anything worth putting on paper. That's when we can make a great tool available to us—the deadline. What's remarkable about a deadline, or an assignment (not necessarily one that someone else gives you, but one you can give to yourself) is that it can serve to awaken what is already inside. Sometimes when I'm writing, when things are going well, I can feel as if there's another voice inside me.

Sometimes it's just working and staying with the work. When I was writing this I wrote one sentence and was ready to give up, but then I wrote a second sentence, and a third. I kept at it. It's the lesson I always need to learn, and teach myself over and over.

Working with a deadline or with some parameters that I've defined before I've begun to make a piece allows me to approach the material in a different way. A few years ago I was observing the potter Chris Staley teach a workshop at Haystack. For one of his assignments he asked the students to each make a dozen cups in the afternoon, and each one of them had to be different. It's a simple idea, but one that can push a maker into new territory. It made me wish that I had studied with Chris when I was making pots. Back then my tendency would be to make the form I knew I could make, the one I was comfortable with. The kind of assignment that Chris gave left comfort behind and opened a world of possibilities.

Last summer I was a participant in a writing workshop led by Betsy Sholl. One afternoon Betsy asked us to write odes to an object. She was basing this on odes by Pablo Neruda that celebrated simple things. At the time of the workshop I was not in the most celebratory of moods. I had recently slipped while walking along the rocky shore and fell about six feet onto my face, on a granite boulder, fracturing my cheekbone. The event was on my mind and the assignment gave me the impetus to write about the fall, not something I would ordinarily think to celebrate.

The Body Remembers

I slip on the rocks at low tide
floating for a timeless moment

over the skeletons of shells, the fields
of barnacles, until my face meets the granite

and my cheek and eye
grow numb and turn blue

and black as my body sets about to heal
the damaged tissue, the broken bone.

To think all this is programmed inside me,
never called on until this moment of swelling

and bleeding. My body, my faithful companion,
my inside out, my outside in, repairs itself

while I sit on top of it, like some incompetent
ruler whose aides know how to take care of all the details.

My body mends itself, like a fisherman at his nets,
like my mother-in-law darning socks. Our job on earth

is to repair the broken and bruised world.
We fix from within, we pull into the garage of the soul

and put ourselves on the lift, take out the
wrenches and grease gun and get to work.

O miraculous recovery!
O what we don't know that blesses us!

There are times when an idea jumps out at you and you know
you to need to communicate it. There are other times, though,
when there are ideas and images floating inside you and you
need to grab one or a few and get started. When we're working
creatively, we can discover the world inside us and join this to
the world outside ourselves. Anything can be the subject for
our art and our creative lives; it's a matter of our willingness to
go deeply into it.

I didn't always think that way. I used to wait for the inspiring moment, for the kind of electrifying event that would be the genesis of the poem. And, while those moments—a call to create—exist, there are other ways to get to those moments. A number of years ago a writer friend suggested a book to me about writing. It's called *Writing Without Teachers* by Peter Elbow. The premise of the book is that we can't be writers and editors at the same time. First you need to generate the material, without judging. Then when it's all out, you can go back in and make decisions about it. That idea opened up my writing. I used to write in a much more self-conscious way—with myself as editor looking over my shoulder—or imagining what my readers—whoever they might be—would be thinking as I wrote a bad sentence. Instead I just decided to let it rip. It was a liberating moment for me, to begin to write not by thinking about what outcome I wanted, but instead by thinking "What have I got to lose?" I found myself reaching a deeper place as I wrote.

Whatever the process I use to get at the words inside me—whether by assignment, or observation or imagination or any combination of these—at some point I will always confront my expectations. We all know expectations, particularly if we're involved in a process with materials. There is the pot as it went into the kiln and there's the way it looks when it comes out. Sometimes it's not what we were expecting and we are disappointed. Other times it has changed in a way that can delight us. And there is the middle ground—the piece didn't meet our expectations, and perhaps we need to drop what we were expecting and look at what is. The lessons we can learn in creating are endless. Knowing your glazes and knowing your kiln helps. But every time we create we're making a new world—however small—that didn't exist. It's not just a world of ideas either, it's a world where we combine our ideas with specific materials—in my case words—and we can't and shouldn't predict the results.

Each act of creativity is an exploration into the unknown. The faith in the act of creating is that when we put the words on the page or the marks on the paper or our hands to the clay that there will be something that's worth saying, that we can make a discovery that will lift us and, we hope, others as well. That's why we're alive and why we have a desire to create.

I was first asked to speak to you early last September. It's hard at this moment to write the word September without seeing the number 11 after it. It has come to be a date for us in the United States and other parts of the world as well, that represents a changed world. For some of us it has made it difficult to think about creativity or the creative process. What's the point, when we have witnessed how quickly creation's opposite—destruction—works. I decided to look up the word create in the dictionary, and one definition of create is "producing through imaginative effort." We who are engaged in the arts are not alone in being imaginative, but we can imagine something and bring it into being.

We can see the world as a hopeless and despairing place, where not just the events of September 11 can confront us, but daily we could learn more than we would ever want to know about poverty and starvation, illiteracy and violence. Perhaps we can observe what is, and begin to create something else.

I haven't completed a poem since September 11. I've written a few short essays about that day and its aftermath. The impact for me has been too gigantic to respond to right now. But I can feel that I'm poised at the water's edge again, ready to take the leap.

When Communism fell in the early 1990s, I learned that the regime of Romanian dictator Nicolae Ceausescu used to register typewriters. Think of words as having so much power that a regime wanted to know everyone who had access to a machine that could produce them! What we confront in our culture when we embark on our creative process is that no one may care about anything that we do. I would not want to have to live in a totalitarian regime to have a sense of urgency in what I need to write. But we should endeavor to have that sense of urgency—that we are contributing in some way to transforming not just ourselves, but our world. Imagination can be a powerful tool and it should be in the service of something. The process of creating allows us to re-imagine the world, to re-envision the world. As makers we realize that not every attempt will succeed, and we also realize that in creating we're drawing from a deeper source that's within us and beyond us at the same time.

* * * *

There are times when I'm writing that I feel I can get beyond my own judgment, even my own intent, and find myself in a new place that is within me and outside myself at the same time. Creating is a journey. It's as if each time we are making something, investigating an idea or a memory, that we have gone into another world, and we come back to this world changed.

The first story in the Bible is the story of creation, and it begins, in the English translation, "In the beginning God created heaven and earth." The Hebrew phrase is *beressheet*, which means beginning. The article "the" is not included—the article is implied, and the rabbis teach us that we could just as easily say in a beginning as in the beginning, the point being that there are many beginnings and that this was just one of them. Perhaps that's the way to see the process by which we create. Each beginning creates something that didn't exist before and in each beginning we can learn and be transformed by the journey. And if it's good we can keep it and if not, we can always start on another piece. It's all inside us and each new piece carries with it everything we've tried and thought before.

At Haystack, the school I direct, we clean out the studios in between every session. There's a remarkable momentum to the sessions. People arrive from all over the country and abroad, people not knowing one another, and then they spend two or three weeks working day and night making work. Everyone's away from home, and it allows us to try new ideas, perhaps liberated by not being where everyone knows who we are. And then that group leaves, full of ideas for new work that will be a part of a continuing creative process. For a day until the next group arrives, the studios are empty and we clean up and begin to get ready again. I love that moment of cleaning up, before we start over again. For me it's a metaphor for our own creative process. We're never finished. We're finished with a project perhaps, and then we're ready to start over again. We're ready to make discoveries, be both disappointed and surprised, and in some way renewed by the process.

Dust Broom in the Studio

Yellow nylon bristles
brown with the residue
of dirt, those motes
of dust that pile up
to make the chaos
that always surrounds us.
The ends of the bristles
look like a cross section
of a fiber optic network,
the communication between
floor and dustpan.
O what amazing things
it has swept up:
the luminescent green
wings of a Luna moth,
eons old stones
that have traveled
in the grooves of our sneakers,
the inner light
of fluorescent tubes,
the crumpled, the broken, the windblown
things of this material world.
Its handle holds the hands
of all who clean,
all who dream of the empty space
all who are ready to begin again.

Art and Community:
Discovery and Rejuvenation
Keynote Speech Glass Art Society, 2003

Whenever I travel, as all of us did to get here, I'm more aware of my community because I'm separated from it. But have you ever felt a moment of lightness when traveling, when, instead of having people look past you or through you, and you doing the same with them, there is a moment when you are actually speaking to one another. You help another person with luggage and make a connection with another human. You realize that you are in some small way in a relationship with another person, which is what is at the center of community.

If a community is "a group of people having common interests," the world of travel, where people are thinking more about where they've been or where they're going, is the opposite of that. When we enter the world of the airport, we're disconnected. We eat mysterious food that has journeyed from some distant kitchen to our airplane tray top. We move through airports that could be anywhere, walking past souvenirs, which are meant to represent what is local, and therefore be about the community, but are generic. They're someone's marketable idea of community. Nothing feels real.

I began my conference journey yesterday in this way, leaving my home in my community in the pre-dawn and driving 60 miles to begin the day of travel to reach this other community, gathered here for a few days, on the other side of our vast and sprawling country, flying over communities that each have their own lives and vitality.

1

I live in the small town of Deer Isle, Maine. There are 3,000 people who live on the island year-round. It's small enough and isolated enough that I am able to observe its workings and for me it has become both a symbol of community and also teaches me about how communities work. As with all communities there are many facets. We have lobstermen, clam diggers, carpenters, plumbers, electricians, writers, potters, and teachers. We have families that have lived here for generations, we have people who spent summers here in their youth who have retired here, we have back-to-the-land people who moved here in the 1970s and have taken root raising families and growing middle aged, we have people who have just purchased shorefront property to build expensive and large second homes. We have year-round residents and summer people. I've lived on the island for 14 years; in some places that would make me an old-timer, but many people on the island can trace their ancestry back many generations. However long I'll live on the island, I'll always be "from-away."

Deer Isle is connected to the mainland by a bridge, but there is still a sense of being an island, which implies a kind of independence, where because we are alone, we are also responsible for one another. Everyone on the island is in some way responsible for everyone else. People recognize this at public gatherings, like the Island's Fourth of July parade, which includes fire trucks from the two volunteer fire departments, floats from the Island daycare center, nursing home, bank, scout troops and others. While it's an event in the summer in an area visited by many tourists, at heart it's a recognition of the island. The parade moves down the small main street of the town, turns around at the site of the old elementary school, and comes back again. It's as if we want to savor the sense of community a second time. What we want to savor is that people can look after one another and take care of one another; everyone is responsible for everyone else.

That same connection is manifested driving around the island, where you meet many practitioners of the Deer Isle wave. I'm not an anthropologist, but I can give you a brief run down of my observations of its use.

It's the hand lifted off the steering wheel when passing another vehicle. It's practiced in a few ways: two fingers of one hand off the wheel, four fingers, occasionally the entire hand can come off the wheel for close friends or family members. One variation, usually practiced by old timers, is the hand off the wheel, moving forward, almost in a lurch. I think I may like this style the best; it's a motion that suggests a blessing or benediction in its own rough way.

Perhaps this wave came from the fishing and boating heritage of the island, as fishermen and sailors are much more apt to recognize what common purpose they have with one another compared to drivers of cars and pickup trucks. I've grown to love waving. To me it stands for what we have in common with one another. It says simply that you are here and I am here and we have some common purpose; we live here together and depend on one another in some way.

A lobster fisherman has told me that out on the water, whatever your view or personal feelings about someone are, you know at some point that you might need their help or they might need yours. It starts, in a sense, out of survival. When I first moved to the island, my family and I returned from a few days away to a winter storm that had dropped over a foot of snow. Our driveway hadn't been plowed yet, so we parked our car on the side of the road to unload from our trip. In the five minutes before it became clear that we were unloading our car and not stuck, four cars had stopped to ask if we needed help with our vehicle.

When one of the high school teams returns on the school bus from a regional or state competition, they are frequently greeted at the bridge by a few fire engines and treated to a round the island parade. People flick their door lights on and off as the parade passes by.

Small communities, have strengths and weaknesses. It's wonderful that everyone knows who you are and what you do, but that also means that the way the people relate to you and what they expect you are capable of is determined by what they already know about you and your family. In a community that surrounds you, if people can't look at you with new eyes, then it's difficult at times to become who you want to be. Think about all the stories that begin with someone leaving the town where they grew up to discover who they really are.

This is one community of which I'm a part. It's my physical community. Each of us is a part of many communities, intersecting circles of interest, need, and support.

2

Haystack is a community also. A small town of artists that's perched on granite ledge. Its vitality is rooted in both its sense of place and in the focus and sense of purpose of the people who gather there. People arrive from all over this country and abroad and become a community. I've had a chance to observe this phenomenon many times. A group of strangers gathers and in a short while—hours and days—it finds its common purpose and becomes a community. We share meals together, we work side by side in studios together, and we share in each other's discoveries—our successes and our failures.

People who come to Haystack and form a community for a brief period of two or three weeks find that it can have depth that is profound. We are away from the small stuff that we all sweat, we are away from the phone that rings, the emails that arrive, the news that assaults us, and we find a place where—other than the roar of the glory holes or the metalsmiths hammering—the world grows quiet and we can discover within ourselves a voice we were waiting to hear. We can hear ourselves think—it can be frightening to hear your own voice, challenging to listen to what it says, but exhilarating too, to reach within and discover we're still there, still alive. While this can happen when we're walking in the woods by ourselves, the amplification and support that community provides creates a kind of mutual energy. Everyone is there with a common sense of purpose—to learn, to try something new—and if we fail, it's a place we are allowed to fail.

This is an intentional community. No one is there because they were born there or their job brought them there. People seem to set out on a journey and arrive at a community like this. They arrive in some sense when the time is right. I'll ask people how they heard about the school and many times the answer is word-of-mouth—a friend told me, a teacher told me, someone I share a studio with spoke about it.

If in a small town everyone one knows who you are and expects certain things from you, at a retreat like Haystack, or

Pilchuck or Penland, you can reimagine who you are. A more traditional community gives you a role to fulfill; at a retreat you leave behind many of your roles from your everyday life, and can discover and mine a deeper source without expectation.

People may arrive with one view of themselves and depart ready to leave their day job to work at their art full time, or head back to school. Doors open that were closed and people sometimes embark on paths that lead them to other communities.

3

Communities preserve things—a way of working, a way of seeing. When I first moved to Deer Isle, I'd left a community where I could walk to the synagogue and we became, as far as I could tell, the only Jewish family on the island, with no synagogue within miles.

In December of the first year that I moved to the island, on a gray day that was spitting snow, I was walking across the main street of the town from the post office to the grocery store. There in the middle of the street I saw a Hasidic Jew walking toward the post office. I thought I was having a vision, as if my Jew had walked out of Eastern Europe of the 19th century to guide me in his long gray beard and black overcoat. When I walked back to the post office, I didn't know the postmaster well enough to ask if a bearded Hasid had just walked in to mail a letter, and by then my man had vanished. I later found out he had a summer home in a town nearby across the bridge, but for me at that moment I took it as a sign, an angelic vision that I wasn't alone.

I discovered as a Jew in Eastern Maine I'm part of a far-flung community. It's centered in Bangor, a sixty-mile drive from my home, and draws congregants from an area even wider than that. It's an effort, to be sure, to maintain those connections, but in some way because there are so few people, perhaps there's a greater sense of responsibility in ensuring the congregation's survival.

A few years ago my rabbi asked me to chant from the Torah as part of our Sabbath service. I was a student again. I learned to decipher the trope marks that accompany the text, I practiced time and again singing along with a tape that the rabbi had made.

When I stood before the congregation, or just before I began, I became as nervous as a young man approaching the Torah for the first time, even though I am accustomed to reading poems to people, talking to groups of people. Then I began to think that this singing is not about me—not how well I do, if I'm in tune or not—but about the ritual I was performing for my community. I was carrying forward an ancient tradition, thousands of years old, to my own community of worshippers. It should have made me more nervous, but it really made me less nervous, because it's not a performance, it's an act in service of something greater than myself.

As makers in our contemporary culture, we sometimes may have no sense of who our audience is or what our work means to them. What we do and the things we make are often not central to our cultural life. My chanting was a moment when what I did was central to the small community in the synagogue.

How often we make things that are not in the service of something greater. While our work may emanate from discoveries that we make about ourselves, we need to make those discoveries be larger than just us. How often we can make work that calls attention to ourselves rather than calling attention to what is sacred or holy and that is outside of us and within us at the same time. We have the capacity to make work for those around us that unites us to one another and to a larger and more profound world.

The rituals that were once central to our lives have been diluted. At times this has brought us greater freedom—where we can live, how we can live, with whom we can live—but we also feel less grounded because of it. In galleries we can see art that implies ritual, but it's not grounded in any culture, in any society, in any community. People make this work because of a yearning to have rituals that reflect our lives and our communities. It's a challenge to us as makers to create things that unite us to our lives.

4

I'm also part of a community of writers. Much like the Deer Isle wave, perhaps we only nod to each other from time to time, to acknowledge that we share the same purpose, we are working with the same materials, and that we share a common heritage. Writers work in more isolation than glass blowers—there aren't teams of poets making poems together, although it's an interesting thought to try it—but we share a belief in the power of words to transform and alter our perceptions.

So communities are wonderful organisms, they support us, they help us to know who we are and where we are. They give order to our worlds.

It's a basic human yearning to be in community. A few years ago my wife, youngest son, and I traveled to Italy and for part of our stay we visited master glassblower Lino Tagliapietra and his family. Venice is a remarkable city that is beautiful, worn, and dreamlike—as if there were an entire way to build cities—water cities—that seems impossible and, because you are afloat there, possible at the same time. The pace of tourism is relentless; it's hard to get a handle on where the real Venice is in Venice, not the souvenir Venice, but some heartbeat of the city. When we spent a few days with Lino and his family—shopping in the market—stopping at many vendors to get different vegetables and seafood, meeting family members and co-workers, we began to feel a sense of place, a sense of community. We got lost on our way back to Lino's house, and when we were able to communicate in our poor Italian where we wanted to go, one person walked us part way to the house and enlisted another to take us the rest of the way. It was the same feeling as being on Deer Isle. Finding a sense of place—rootedness—is when I feel most alive. People are connected to the place where they live and the place and the people are in a relationship, an organism.

5

The smallest community I've been in was for five minutes on a subway in New York City. Subways are a place where conversation with a stranger, other than to ask directions, can feel at least inappropriate if not scary. Once, though, I was standing next to a blind man who was seated with his guide dog. His dog began to eat a tissue on the floor and three of us who were traveling near him pointed that out. He thanked us, and we talked until the next stop about breeds of dogs and their habits.

The largest community I've experienced was the United

States in the months following September 11th. The sense of common purpose and mourning in our country and the honoring of the victims, drew us together as a national community.

My brother was one of those who perished in the World Trade Center. The support that I witnessed first hand, from people I've known well and from people I've only met a few times, has been profound. What struck me when our family was in mourning was that community doesn't exist only in small towns where everyone can wave to one another; it is the very network of our humanity. My brother and his wife and daughter lived in an older suburb in New Jersey. One of the nights after he died, my sister-in-law looked outside her house to see people from her neighborhood standing in a candlelight vigil surrounding her home. At their best, communities can encircle us in light like that.

And at our best, we can give light back to our communities. At my brother's memorial service his friends and co-workers would talk about how he had given back to the community he lived in~in the small ways that are the biggest ways of all—visiting the elderly, working in a homeless shelter, visiting the sick, advising people as they sought direction in their lives. The power within a community is that we support it as it supports us.

In the months following the World Trade Center horror, the New York Times published Portraits in Grief, brief descriptions of the lives of those who had perished in those buildings. Each life was part of a community and the Times chose not to recognize the professional achievements of those who perished, but rather focused on what they did with their lives—their relationships with co-workers, with relatives, with the lives each led within their varied and diverse communities.

It felt for a moment that because we had the capacity to recognize and cherish those lives within those buildings—firefighter, police officer, stockbroker, janitor, restaurant worker, secretary—that we could begin to see each life as precious and to see each life torn from its own community. It seemed that we could see this extend beyond a city, a region and a country and see a world of communities, each with lives to be cherished. What a symbol the World Trade Center could have become then, a tragedy that would help us see the common bonds that could unite all humans. Tragically and sadly, our leaders have taken it as an opportunity to define some communities as worthwhile and others as not.

6

I am part of all these communities and they inform who I am. The community that comprises the Glass Arts Society has something in common with all the communities I've mentioned. In many ways the world of glass, in Seattle and elsewhere, is a small town—everyone knows everyone, people depend on one another for support and even to make their work. People who work in glass understand its heritage, its lineage, and when they are creating work, carry it forward in some way. Of all the communities of craft media/visual artists, the glass community has the greatest sense of mutual dependence. At the same time that glass workers are kind of a small town, your community is also an international community. Your friendships and working relationships span countries and continents. In a world that grows more divided, your community is also a symbolic one—it represents ways that we can understand one another through art.

Communities are constantly changing, and today, with increased travel, trade, and communication, the identities of communities can change rapidly. The coastal property in Maine is bought by people who want to build lavish second homes. How is that absorbed into the life of a small town? Tourism in cities, towns and villages, where visitors are initially attracted to the vitality of a community can make that community, as it puts itself on display, become a caricature of itself.

No community is isolated anymore in the way it was even 25 years ago. The challenge, as we become less isolated is to also maintain those attributes that give our local lives significance. But we also need to see that we are part of much larger communities. Now we are in a world where we are beginning to understand that community goes beyond people and place and that place relies on the health of its environment. If the waters around Deer Isle aren't healthy, then fishing isn't healthy, and if fishing isn't healthy then the community isn't either. Our communities are much larger than human communities.

When the Apollo astronauts took a photograph of the earth from space and for the first time we could see ourselves all floating on one small planet together, many people commented that this represented a shift in our thinking, that we were in a sense a global community. From that heavenly vantage point, you can see that we are a closed system—we share the same resources, we breathe the same air, we float in the same water.

But at the same time our consciousness has shifted to embrace this notion, and the internet has connected us to one another in ways that were unimaginable even 10 years ago, we're also confronted more and more with a world that's completely disconnected. We're disconnected from the sources of our food, we're disconnected from how things are made, we're disconnected from one another in our own country—where we can drive from place to place in our car and never have to relate to another person—and we're isolating ourselves in the world. American influence certainly spreads everywhere, and people from many countries may speak English, but we're not talking the same language.

So, what does all this have to do with people who make glass and live in Seattle or have traveled to Seattle? Makers, people who work with materials and see processes from start to finish, are wonderful examples of how we can connect both to our communities and our world. Our lack of connection to so many elements in our world is what makes us yearn for community. Makers have an intuitive connection to the processes and materials of creation. We are buoyed by the act of creation, buoyed by the supportive community that honors the creative process. From my brief visits in Seattle, I can see that the creativity of the glass community has inspired others, and inspired a spirit of the community as well.

Your community extends beyond Seattle. In a world where there seems to be more distrust and hate, you are positioned to be ambassadors for something outside yourself. Your international focus creates understanding.

The arts build communities and reflect the life of the community. It's not enough to have an arts community that congratulates itself. We need to seek ways to be part of our larger communities. Like families, communities carry forward the past to the future. Just the way we can recognize the face of our ancestors in our children, there is a kind of code that communities carry forward, information we carry within ourselves that provides continuity to our lives where we live. But no communities are standing still, nor should they be. All are changing and evolving. We can't keep things the way they used to be, but we can honor the past and see what from the past we want to carry with us to the future.

As I began to consider this topic, I thought at first of the communities that support me and that I'm a part of—my own town, the art center where I work, my synagogue that provides me with some spiritual and cultural grounding, and writers and artists with whom I speak about making work. It occurred to me that all those attributes are also present in artists like you who are pursuing a craft. While each community is unique, each community is universal as well. We are all tied to our particular geographies and to those groups and people who make us whole.

If we only support our own community, though, to the exclusion of others, then community can separate us instead of uniting us. Extremists and terrorists are kinds of communities too, but they lack the empathy that makes us realize that each community, each life, is part of a larger community.

7

A few years ago Haystack was invited to participate in a nationwide project with the Liz Lerman Dance Exchange. Liz had conceived of the Hallelujah Project, where her company would go into communities—large ones like Tucson and Minneapolis and Los Angeles and small ones like Deer Isle—and listen to the stories of those places and ask people what they wanted to praise, and made dances about those things they were "in praise of."

On Deer Isle the dancers visited and spoke with people and were in residence for two weeks. We developed a dance that was the inaugural performance at a 400-seat theater at the new elementary school on the island. There were 10 dancers from the company joined by 40 dancers from the community. The youngest was 6 and the oldest was 97. We performed for a capacity crowd, helping the community to celebrate itself. What a powerful experience to make art that supports your own community.

As makers we need to seek similar roles that are central to those places where we live and dream.

Thinking Inside the Box:
Creativity, Compassion and Community

William Jamison Lecture, Oregon College of Art and Craft/Pacific Northwest College of Art
February 27, 2005

When I began to prepare for this talk we were visiting with a friend in her apartment in Phoenix. It was a beautiful home, everything was so well thought out in terms of design. Every detail was attended to, from the passages between rooms, how artwork was displayed, how the outside looked from the inside. It was a space that made you feel elevated to be in it. We had a beautiful lunch, of bread and cheese that were produced locally and bought from a local vendor who knew our friends. Staying with my friend was her mother—93 years old and using a walker—to move slowly around this space. She had lunch with us and was moving in a slower time, moving in a space where the options are increasingly more limited, where a journey from one room to another might be enough for a day. She moved fluidly between now and then—we were visitors who would soon be forgotten, but she engaged us with her eyes and told us about the things she had planted in her yard with her husband and how she would sometimes pay boys in the neighborhood to help her out with the gardening. We left our friends' beautiful home, where at least for a moment, the past and the present were flowing together, and drove to see some galleries. In Phoenix everything spreads out, the only order imposed by the grid of roads. For a traveler it's a hard city to feel grounded in—where architecture or landmarks would give you sense of place.

We were surrounded by the arid mountains that hold the city in. Millions of years ago this was a shallow sea and that day we drove in the dry ocean bed to Scottsdale where we looked at galleries. We walked into a gallery that has some pretty pricey work—a $225,000 painting and a sculpture made of found wood for $170,000. We made the comparisons to how large a house we could build with the proceeds from the sale of the painting.

There's something about seeing a price tag like that that focuses your attention on meaning, value, and worth. An hour before we'd been talking to a woman who had lived for almost a century, telling us about digging trenches in her back yard to plant fruit trees. Hundreds of millions of years ago, we're treading water in the ocean.

We make our way to the Scottsdale Art Center where there's an exhibition of the work of the Rural Studio and it's founder, Samuel Mockbee. There are photographs of ingenious projects in rural Hale County, Alabama; projects that make use of very little to make spaces for worship, for living, for community, for play. A chapel is made of recycled tires. The glass front of a community center is made from recycled windshields from Chevrolet Caprices. Anything, it seems, can be used to make a building possible—old tin, glass, straw, waxed cardboard boxes—are transformed.

In one art space, we see work that is clearly a commodity, whatever its original purpose. I feel about it the way that I feel about professional athletes. There is a demonstration of remarkable skill and grace, but something is clearly out of whack when a baseball player gets paid thousands of dollars every time he gets a base hit. In another art space, we see work that is rooted in a community, work that gives the community a greater sense of purpose. Feeling surrounded by the geology of the southwest, I reflect on how ancient our surroundings are, and how briefly we humans have been here. It puts all our efforts into a different perspective as well.

These are some of the things I think about when I contemplate what it means to be creative in our society. We associate creativity with the arts, but surely its reach is broader and deeper. As I'm writing this, the man comes to plow our driveway after a snowstorm. It's a heavy snow and he has to back up repeatedly on our pitched dirt driveway. Certainly there's creativity between his foot and the clutch, his hands and the plow. It's a small moment, but I wouldn't be able to get out of my driveway without it. I also couldn't get out of my driveway if our saintly mechanic didn't know how to tinker with old engines.

Often calling something creative becomes our stock response to those things we can't understand. Our corrupt corporate bookkeeping is "creative accounting." Our relatives say, "You're so creative," responding to our latest effort. Our world is full of people who can make and do things with great creativity and skill. Always in our culture, creativity and commerce mix together.

What does it mean to create? According to Webster's Third International Dictionary, it ranges from "To bring into existence: make out of nothing and for the first time" (God created the heaven and the earth) to the British slang meaning to complain loudly, carry on or gripe (as in "don't go near him when he's creating."). There are a number of definitions in between, but perhaps those parameters help define the process by which we're creating, or at least how we see ourselves at our highest and lowest points. At one moment we can't believe something could emerge of such power that we're even a part of it. At the next moment, we're lost and whining to ourselves, hoping to find the way again.

Let's reserve the first definition, "to make out of nothing and for the first time," for God alone. Here on earth, we know that we're in a closed system and everything is created from something else: trees become earth, stone becomes clay, and our ideas grow and change from our connection with others. Every act of creativity is a kind of partnership. Working with materials is a partnership: iron behaves in a certain way, clay in another. We observe how material responds and we respond. We make discoveries. The same form made of clay, iron, or reeds will have a different voice and a different use. The words that I'm choosing now, each one after another, have their own voice too. Their rhythms, how they move in the mouth, the lineage of the culture from which they've traveled, and their current life.

Creativity is humans being alive in the world and responding to it. One human urge is to create, to make. We feel that connection when we learn of our ancestors, millennia ago, shaping rock for the first time. Another human impulse is to categorize. We collect things in specific ways: we have museums for science and natural history and art and craft and design. We make and observe and then we separate. It's a useful way for us to organize the world and not be overwhelmed by its messy abundance. Often, though, I wish that we could gather everything in museums that would join the world together, with names like "The Museum of Wonderful Things" or "The

Institute of Amazing Objects and Ideas." Too often we're making barriers when we should be having conversations.

This sometimes makes us construct divisions between ways of being creative. A few years ago at Haystack we held a symposium in conjunction with the MIT Media Lab. We called the event "Digital Dialogues: Technology and the Hand" and our aim was to examine the world of new technology—the new digital—and the digits of our hands. We wanted to look at how we make things and the role that the hand can still have in this new world. Our invited audience included artists, craftspeople, educators, philosophers, researchers, scientists, and writers.

When I visited the Media Lab in Cambridge for our planning sessions, I was taken with the spirit of creativity that was a part of the place. It had the messy chaos of an artists' studio or a teenager's room.

We were two different worlds, though, one rural and craft, the other urban and high tech. In one of our first planning meetings, when we were deciding on the next date to meet, I was the only one who had a paper calendar—all the others were electronic. And as we discussed our list of invitees—half of whom would be people working in digital media—I was worried about how we might all get along.

As part of the design of the symposium, we had organized some of the studios to have a person with a technology background working with a person with a craft background. These two people would collaborate in some way—we weren't sure of the outcome and didn't have any expectations, but we knew that we wanted a significant part of the symposium to be hands on. One of these collaborations was between blacksmith Tom Joyce from Santa Fe, New Mexico and Justine Cassell, professor in the Gesture and Narrative Language Group at the Media Lab. They were assisted at various times by four or five others. What Tom and Justine created was a forged steel vessel that told the story, through video and audio, of its own making. As you would reach inside the vessel, you could pull out the sounds or images, which were triggered by motion sensors. Watching this team work together, using technologies that ranged from the ancient mythic fires of the blacksmith to the cool media of the digital camera and LED lights, I was impressed with the tenacity with which everyone worked, from hammering steel to writing computer programs. I began to see not people who were worlds apart, but a continuum of creativity, and the remarkable human capacity to solve problems with the tools that are available.

Because we have made so many rapid advances in the digital world, we sometimes equate "technology" with "new," but it's really the most ancient of human stories. And what is technology but the manifestation of our creativity. Our challenge now is to create technology that makes us more human, more in touch—both through our hands and minds—with ourselves and the world around us.

Creativity doesn't exist by itself. It's always in relationship to something—a problem we are trying to solve or a question we are trying to answer. Thomas Edison said, "To invent you need a good imagination and a pile of junk." This is a sentiment that could unite mechanics, engineers, scientists, and artists. You're probably familiar with the scene from the movie Apollo 13 when the three astronauts in the disabled lunar module need to build an apparatus that will remove the carbon dioxide from the capsule. A team on the ground is given only what's available on board—cardboard, plastic hose, duct tape—and a very limited amount of time, to figure out how to build something when people's lives are at stake. If this group had a year to work and all the resources they needed at their disposal, who knows what they would have come up with, or how many hours of meetings they would have sat through. The limitations, the immediacy, and sense of purpose were the catalysts for creativity.

A few years ago I visited the Whitney Museum in New York, not to see a particular show, and wandered into a remarkable exhibition of the Quilts of Gees Bend. These are quilts made by African American women in an isolated community in rural Alabama, and some of the most visually stunning visual work that I'd ever seen. The elements that comprised the quilts included mattress ticking, scraps from their husbands' old overalls and shirts. It had all the visual sophistication of abstract art and the implicit necessity of something that was made for use. It had elements of African heritage and jazz improvisation. Oftentimes I can find myself looking at art and puzzling about intent or trying to understand—in short, I find myself working at it. This was like falling in love. There was no question that something deeply creative and essential was going on here.

It's ironic, of course, that I would see essentially community-based work in a major American museum. These were pieces that were made by the community for the community. I thought of the hierarchy that we've created in the visual arts, that often puts painting first, perhaps painting by men first, and then see this handwork as further down the ladder. What was moving about these works is that they were rooted in community and that they had their roots in necessity.

Our lives now are not so much about survival. In a sense

we've outsourced our survival—someone will grow our food, build our shelters, provide fuel to heat our homes, so that we've lost that moment when our own creativity and ingenuity were essential to our living. When we are creating, that is the very energy, the very vision that we need to recapture.

To create anything that works we need a combination of skill and inspiration. That's what happened to the scientists who built the carbon dioxide exchanger in Apollo 13. We need to know what we're working with—whether the material is clay or words—and how it responds. But in any creative process, from scientific discovery to religious quest—we have to be willing to get lost. We have to go somewhere where we don't know answers, and where we are not sure of our results.

A few years ago I was listening to the National Public Radio show Fresh Air and the host, Terry Gross, was interviewing the Catholic writer and theologian John Dominic Crosen. I'm remembering now it was Easter time, and they were talking about the life of Jesus. Crosen was describing the symbolic nature of Jesus' life. "Are you saying the virgin birth is just a metaphor," Terry Gross asked, and I inferred in her voice a chance to separate the literal from the figurative. Crosen thought for a moment and agreed that it was indeed a metaphor, but not just a metaphor, the modifier that she had chosen, for metaphor, he said, is the most powerful tool that humans have. Metaphor is our way of seeing when we are creative—we are joining things together in a way that didn't exist before—we are making one thing out of two things or three things. Metaphors can elevate us and take our breath away.

When a metaphor works it joins things together in a way that is unexpected and yet absolutely right at the same time. We live in the world we see and also in the world that we imagine and perhaps metaphor is the place in between.

There is a wonderful metaphor that I came across in a book called The Jew in the Lotus by Rodger Kamanetz. It documents a visit to India by a group of rabbis and Jewish thinkers, who were invited by the Dalai Lama, who was interested in learning how cultures and religions can survive for thousands of years in exile. In it Zalman Schacter describes Rabbi Yitzhak Luria, who was a great Kabbalist of the 1500s. Schacter says that the rabbi

"taught that in the first part of creation God made the light and made vessels for the light. The vessels were too fragile, they broke and from the broken vessels of the supernal lights the material world was created. So when I sit in this chair with mindfulness, the spark of God that's in it gets raised. It all begins with a cosmic catastrophe, because bringing energy from the infinite to the finite is very hard. Even God had to try a few times in creation, and the first few times it didn't quite work in the way in which it needed to be, according to the Lurianic tradition. And it says that God creates worlds and destroys them. So depending on where the spark was in the great scheme of things, it falls down and then has to go up and be raised. It's the purpose of human beings to find the sparks here and raise them up."

The rightness of this metaphor for me is that often when we are at our most creative, we feel we are in collaboration, somehow, with the project we are working on—that we are uncovering something that existed before or we are bringing clarity to something that was always there. Any creative act is a partnership between the maker and the material, how it responds, how it moves, and how we respond to it. There is a rhythm to creativity too, when we are completely involved in our task; it's as if we're in another time. When I was a potter one of my favorite moments was after the pots were made in the morning and I could look at a shelf of still wet vessels, as if they'd just been born, and see the emptiness that they contained. I had made a space that was defining space. Or I should say that the clay and I together had created this, for what would it be without clay and even with the two of us working together, there was still some other force—that space, that breath inside the pot—that was beyond us.

While sometimes metaphor can open up a way of seeing for us, it can also slip easily into an image so overused and reliable that it loses its power. When I began to prepare for this talk, I was considering the phrase "thinking outside the box," which implies looking outside of the norm, outside where everyone else at the corporate board table is looking—thinking creatively. And I thought, what about "thinking inside the box" instead? I was thinking about how we live in our own communities and the role that creativity can have in everything that we do. As anyone who has struggled with making something knows, it's easy to inject the "if only" into the process, as in "If only I had this kind of wood," or "If only I had the right kind of light," or "If only I had my own studio," or "If only I had some coffee," as a way of saying that we can't go to work right now. It can become a way of avoiding taking the hard inner journey of creation, of looking within ourselves and our limitations, physical, spiritual, or material—our "box." But the world needs our creativity and we need to get to work right now. And it's good to work within a box, to not save our greatest ideas for some other moment or the show at the Museum of Modern Art or the Whitney, but to make in the place where we live in our own communities. It's what made the quilts of Gees Bend so compelling—they were made in relationship to a specific place.

I like the limitation of the box too. Within limits we can make something limitless. All the time and all the tools at our disposal don't guarantee success. According to an article about art in prisons by Guy Trebay in the New York Times last fall, even when all art materials are forbidden, inmates still maintain a tremendous desire to produce objects that are significant to them. They will extract color from M&Ms and shampoo to make tattoos. One inmate salvaged 400 packs of Kool cigarettes to weave a handbag.

What I'm describing are the severest limitations for making. We are fortunate to not be limited in these ways, though and the box I'd like us to think within should be a big one. I'm thinking back to my afternoon in Phoenix when I saw two kinds of art—one, though beautifully executed, having been cut loose from any sense of relationship to place or community, and the other, work that was rooted in a community. Since, ultimately our creativity is tied directly to our survival, we join our creative impulses together. We can create for a world where we are not saying "either/or" but "both/and." We can create things that are significant and we can do this for communities we are a part of.

When I began writing this talk, I made some preliminary notes—shorthand of those things I wanted to remember to say to you. These notes were first and have followed me throughout my writing, they are the sentences just beyond my last sentence—in another time I'd have worked on paper, but this is written on my computer, so just below the phrase I'm on, my reminders would appear. It's like having someone whispering to you all the time, the small voice in your ear. The phrase I wrote was Tikkun Olam, which is a Hebrew phrase which means to repair the world. There is a Jewish teaching that our obligation is to repair this broken world, to make it a better place. We are the ones who must mend and heal. It goes along with finding the broken light of creation. I'm glad that this phrase has followed me, because it's central to what our creativity must be about—scientific or artistic. We don't need to know the outcome, and our best work is probably done when we don't know where exactly it's headed, but we need to work knowing that what we do matters.

A few years ago Kim Stafford was a visiting writer at Haystack. I enjoy when we have visiting writers because it gives me the opportunity to write at a time when it's hard for me to focus on writing. Kim gave us an assignment—an invitation to write he would call it—but one that was a limitation as well. He asked as a warm up that we write a run-on sentence—a way to keep writing and propel the text along using conjunctions like and and but. For me this was an inspiring limitation and over the last few years I've been writing a series of poems that have grown out of the run-on sentence. It was a way for me to move into the unknown. I began to think of them as prayers that were centered in my life at the moment and in the community I live in. It feels like completing a circle to come back to Kim's hometown of Portland, to read these.

Prayer

Our problem – may I include you? – is that we
don't know how to start, how to just close
our eyes and let something dance between
our hearts and our lips, we don't know how
to skip across the room only for the joy of the leap.
We walk, we run, but what happened to the skip
and its partner, the gallop, the useless and imaginary
way we could move through space, the horses we
rode before we knew how to saddle up, before we
had opinions about everything and just loved
the wind in our faces and the horizon in our eyes.

Driving and Going to Work Prayer

Driving across the causeway this morning
I saw the sun rising, only it wasn't a blinding-
in-your-eyes yellow sun, it was a huge
red ball coming up through layers of stratus clouds
a red sun as if it were a science fiction movie
and we had landed on a planet that was almost like earth,
but there were other planets circling us, other suns,
and that's how my morning began, looking for something
miraculous that is always there, the same way Cheryl
was cooking eggs for 100 people and didn't want
to leave them until they began to scramble themselves
into yellow clusters and became breakfast
and who wouldn't want to wait for that because that's
when we are transformed, when we are changed,

and we are ourselves but also becoming something
different, something we didn't know that begins
to change itself, something that's coming, arriving,
returning, like a multiple choice question when the answer
is all of the above, all of the above.

April Prayer

Just before the green begins there is the hint of green
a blush of color, and the red buds thicken
the ends of the maple's branches and everything
is poised before the start of a new world,
which is really the same world
just moving forward from bud
to flower to blossom to fruit
to harvest to sweet sleep, and the roots
await the next signal, every signal
every call a miracle and the switchboard
is lighting up and the operators are
standing by in the pledge drive we've
all been listening to: Go make the call.

Prayer in the Strip Mall, Bangor, Maine

The week after Thanksgiving and the stores are decked out
for holiday shopping including a TJ Maxx where what was
once too expensive loses its value and attracts us, there is a
store with a big yellow banner proclaiming GIANT BOOK SALE,
a seasonal operation of remaindered books, which doesn't mean
that the books aren't good, only that the great machinery
of merchandising didn't engage it's gears in quite the right way
and I buy two books of poetry and am leaving the store, the first
snowstorm
of the winter on the way and as I get to the glass double doors
a bearded man with a cane is entering, he has been walking
with a woman who is continuing on to another store and he
has the look that could make him either eccentrically brilliant
or just plain simple and as I open the door and he opens the other
side
he turns and says "I love you," not to me but calling back to his
friend who is departing, only he's said it looking at me, closest
to me, which is unintended love, random love, love that
should be spread throughout the world, shouted in our ears for
free.

Spring Prayer

The white that appears to be the last remnant
of the snow in the woods is a plastic trash bag
snagged in the undergrowth, as natural a phenomenon
as anything, considering all things come
from something of this earth—you, me, plastic bags,
pebbles, and sand—and we're all moving at our own pace

somewhere, the where of which we haven't figured out yet
and never will, the some of which is the treasure chest
of all we've accumulated, how lovingly we hold
these artifacts in our minds: the photo, the book,
the jewel, the sorrow, the green shoot piercing
last year's fallen leaf.

Headache Prayer

I wake with a headache and watch as the blue jay
who yesterday had a stick in its beak continues
to build its nest and I see it fly from the maples that grew up
in the brush, over the roof to wherever the nest will be,
and for the blue jay it's the start of a day that is in the present
looking toward the future informed by the instinct of the past
from wing to tree to nest to offspring to wing and my pulse
throbs in my head and down into my chest, an ancient
drum that is beating in everything, in the sap in the tree
in the seed in the ground, in the wind on the horizon. Amen.

Ancestor Prayer

The grass is covered with the first crust
of icy snow so that walking across it
I can see the footsteps of those who
have gone before me, like following the paths
of ancestors as if there is some solace
and sanctuary in following those who have
preceded us and I walk to the meditation hall
where high windows show only the branches
and not the trunks of the trees and in this way

we're not seeing the source, but we know
it's there because it supports the branches
that hold the leaves, which today are no longer
there, fallen to the ground, blown into the banks
of the river, carried away on wind and water.

Water Prayer

And this morning I awoke to rain, which makes
its own rhythm on the window, and the world is full
of these rhythms, rhythm of water, rhythm of the heart,
which sounds like an underwater pump, the lub-dub
of all it knows, which is making all I know possible,
and on the roof rain falls and turns to hail, then snow,
then rain again, running down the shingles to the gutter,
the gathering up that makes rivers and lakes and oceans,
from cloud to drop to torrent, how nothing is lost.

So here we are in the battered and bruised world, the one we
have an obligation to mend and repair. What better metaphor
for mending than to think of the quiltmakers of Gees Bend
who I mentioned earlier. Here's what one of them, Geraldine
Westbrook said about their work, "...All us, that's what we
worked at, quilts and stuff. That's all we had to do. You just
had to find a way to do it yourself, out of old clothes, old overalls...we made them out of old clothes, old socks, and then after
people went to work in piece factories, if you had somebody re-
lated they would get you pieces. I don't follow no pattern, I just
went to putting them together, just get me a needle and some
thread and sitting down and just went to work. I was just doing the best I could. When you sit down you got to get yourself

a mind of your own, figure out a way to put them together." (*Quilts of Gees Bend* p. 86.)

Throughout history I'm sure, people have known the fragility of the world, how quickly events can change our lives. Between terrorism, war, and natural disasters we've gone on a journey lately to other places, some darker and deeper, some of great and unimaginable sorrow. It certainly feels as if we're teetering now, less secure, but if we think of ourselves traveling in that world of shattered light, then creation is all around us, waiting of us to discover it.

REFERENCES

The Jew in the Lotus: a Poet's Rediscovery of Jewish Identity in Buddhist India by Rodger Kamenetz (New York: Harper Collins, 1995) p.99.

Guy Trebay "Ingenious Crafts Projects for a Stir-Crazy Day" *New York Times*, September 26, 2004.

The Quilts of Gees Bend by John Beardsley et.al. (Tinwood Books: Atlanta in association with The Museum of Fine Arts, Houston 2002) p. 86.

Photo credits, with thanks